The 11th Element

The 11th Element

The Key to Unlocking Your Master Blueprint For Wealth and Success

ROBERT SCHEINFELD

WILEY

JOHN WILEY & SONS, INC.

Published by John Wiley & Sons, Inc., Hoboken, New Jersey.
Published simultaneously in Canada.

For general information on our other products and services please contact our
Customer Care Department within the United States at 800-762-2974, outside the
United States at 317-572-3993 or fax 317-572-4002.

Wiley also publishes its books in a variety of electronic formats. Some content that
appears in print may not be available in electronic books. For more information about
Wiley products, visit our web site at www.wiley.com.

Library of Congress Cataloging-in-Publication Data:

Scheinfeld, Robert.
  The 11th element : the key to unlocking your master blueprint for
wealth and success / Robert Scheinfeld.
      p. cm.
  Includes bibliographical references and index.
  ISBN 0-471-44413-8 (CLOTH)
  1. Success in business.   2. Success—Psychological aspects.   I. Title:
Eleventh element.   II. Title.
  HF5386.S377   2003
  650.1—dc21

                                                                    2003010881

Printed in the United States of America.

10 9 8 7 6 5 4 3 2 1

CONTENTS

FOREWORD

For 25 years, I've been creating wealth, business success, and multiple streams of income for myself and teaching others to do the same. My experience has taught me that the success process has two components to it: the visible and the invisible.

The visible component includes people, ideas, resources, techniques, and strategies—what you hear about most when you study success.

The invisible component includes the tremendous pool of raw power from which the visible components actually draw. The world's most successful people acknowledge their reliance on invisible forces to produce results. They know that this *invisible world* is the source of whatever abundance they've been able to create.

In my own life, some of my greatest successes came from help I received from the invisible world. Have you ever had a hunch? When part of you knows that something is right even though another part of you is skeptical? Well, I usually listen to my intuition. It was a hunch that inspired me to start investing in real estate in the 1970s just before the huge boom.

It was another hunch that inspired me to leave my career as an investment counselor and write my first book, *Nothing Down*. The odds of a new author getting a book published are 10,000 to 1.

Part of me just knew that if I followed my hunches, something good would happen. How could I have known that *Nothing Down* would become a *New York Times* bestseller? My second book, *Creating Wealth,* was also a bestseller. Then I had a hunch to start several seminar companies. They grossed over $100 million in the next 15 years.

Where did those hunches come from? How and why did I get them? That's just a small part of what you're about to discover— and why I'm so excited about the material Bob shares in this book.

Many how-to books have been written about the visible components of wealth and success. Other books have been written about the invisible components of success. But never before has anyone mapped out the "territory" of the invisible side of success as completely, precisely, and clearly as Bob does in *The 11th Element.*

After mapping out the unseen territory, he continues by providing you with a step-by-step system and toolkit for tapping into the immensely powerful resources available to you there.

Systems and toolkits save you time, energy, and money. All wealthy people have systems or "cookie cutters" they've developed through years of trial and error to cut real "dough" out of their markets and niches. They all have step-by-step formulas they apply repeatedly to produce results.

Armed with your new map, system, and toolkit, you will be empowered to produce, as Bob says, "extraordinary results, in less time, with less effort—and much more fun."

As you'll soon see, Bob has used the map, system, and toolkit presented in this book to produce extraordinary results for himself and a select group of clients. His methods have been applied to create wealth and success through home-based businesses, small businesses, Internet businesses, brick-and-mortar retail businesses, even Fortune 500 businesses.

No matter what your current situation or desire may be, the wisdom you'll receive from this book will transform your world, your finances, and the results you produce on a daily basis.

Bob has cracked the code on how to produce business break-throughs at breakneck speed by tapping into *The 11th Element*. I consider *The 11th Element* to be a must have for all executives, managers, network marketers, and entrepreneurs who want to create and increase their wealth and personal freedom.

ROBERT G. ALLEN
Author of *Nothing Down, Creating Wealth, Multiple Streams of Income, Multiple Streams of Internet Income,* and with co-author Mark Victor Hansen, *The One Minute Millionaire: The Enlightened Way to Wealth.*

INTRODUCTION

It was a sunny Saturday morning in Crans, Switzerland, in August 1969. I was at a café, sipping hot chocolate with a 70-year-old man who had amassed a vast personal fortune after founding and building a multibillion-dollar Fortune 500 company. I welcomed the opportunity to discover the secrets of that kind of extraordinary, monumental success. Finally, he set down his cocoa and said, "You've been peppering me with questions. Now let me tell you the secret. . . ."

I sat with rapt attention for hours as he introduced me to the little-known strategies, mind-set, and tactics he used to found and build Manpower, Inc. into the world's largest temporary help service, accumulating billions in revenue.

"The process of creating wealth includes many elements," he told me. "They're all important, but there's one element that's the glue, the 'master controller' that holds them together and makes them all work. I became a master at working with that little-known element, and when *you* do, the highest levels of business success and wealth can be yours too."

That man was Aaron Scheinfeld, my grandfather.

We talked for hours, my grandfather and I. And over the 12 months that followed, he began teaching me his system for tapping into what I've come to call *The 11th Element* to create business success and wealth.

Why do I call it *The 11th Element?* Because many success and wealth-building systems have been created and offered over the years, and most of them discuss or center around some combination of *10 elements* the authors claim are necessary for creating total success. These 10 elements—desire, belief, the law of attraction, goal setting, modeling, create clear and detailed plans, taking massive action now, persistence, visualization, and affirmations—are certainly important. But they're all missing the one ingredient that's absolutely essential for the creation of business success and wealth—an element that, when managed correctly, virtually guarantees success.

They're all missing *The 11th Element* that my grandfather introduced to me in that Swiss café.

Unfortunately, my grandfather died before I could complete my *11th Element* education. I applied what I learned from him in the years that followed and became a millionaire by the age of 31.

Then, I had a seven-year bout with Murphy's Law, where everything that could go wrong did in my business and financial lives. During those seven years, I lost everything and actually went $153,000 into debt. I didn't understand what was happening to me, and I became very confused and angry. I wasn't able to go to my grandfather and say, "What didn't you tell me?" or "What am I missing?" or "What else do I need to know here?"

I was on my own.

Through those extremely stressful seven years, by applying the core strategies my grandfather taught me, I was able to piece together the other parts of the system. I developed the complete system I use now and applied it to dig myself out of my financial hole, rebuild my career and finances, and soar much higher than I had in my first 31 years—improving my quality of life in the process.

Now it's your turn to find out what I discovered in that Swiss café, the missing pieces I collected during the years I spent with "Murphy," and the numerous refinements I've added to the system by working with it on my own projects, and with clients, associates, and customers.

Let's begin by considering a few questions. Have you ever wondered how some people come up with one winning business idea or venture after another? Or, if that's a skill you have, wondered how you make that skill work for you?

Have you ever wondered how some people always seem to be "in the right place at the right time" to produce amazing results, say "just the right thing" to close the sale, or always find a way to "get the job done," no matter what obstacles they encounter? Some people seem to lead "charmed lives" and have a "knack" for unusual success.

Have you ever imagined the kind of wealth and business success you could create if you only had the right idea, the right plan, access to the right people, the right skills, the right funding and resources, or used the right system?

Surely you've pondered such questions more than once. You're about to discover the untold story and the true nature of what's usually referred to as luck, synchronicity, or "being in the right place at the right time"—and a system you can quickly and easily apply to:

- Start a business
- Build an existing business
- Attract and keep top talent
- Increase your sales, profits, income, and wealth
- Overcome the inevitable challenges you'll encounter along the way

The system for tapping into *The 11th Element* involves mastering four critical skills:

1. Shifting your mind-set so you can access *The 11th Element* and tap into its power
2. Getting clear on what you *really* want (versus what you *think* you want)

3. Tapping into *The 11th Element* to ask for help to produce the results you really want

4. Receiving the help you requested (it's not always as easy as you'd think)

This book reveals how to master and apply these four critical skills, and it illustrates how my grandfather and I, along with other entrepreneurs, applied *The 11th Element* to become wealthy and create lifestyles most people only dream about.

In the early days of my career, I tapped into *The 11th Element* to become a top salesperson for a computer reseller, and I produced extraordinary results as a sales manager, corporate communications manager, regional manager, director of marketing, vice president of marketing, consultant, and entrepreneur. In more recent phases of my career, I applied *The 11th Element* to:

- Create and execute a marketing model that packed rooms at Tony Robbins' multimedia seminars.

- Fuel the growth of a computer store franchise company called Connecting Point of America from $90 million to $350 million in very profitable sales in less than three years.

- Build and run the "marketing machine" that rocketed Blue Ocean Software from $1.27 million to $44.3 million in just four years, resulting in the company being named three times to *Inc.* magazine's Inc. 500 list. That tremendous growth, accompanied by staggering profitability, led to Blue Ocean being acquired by software giant Intuit for $177 million in September 2002.

You'll also discover dozens of examples that illustrate how my clients and associates applied *The 11th Element* to start businesses, build businesses, grow their incomes and net worths, create new careers, write best-selling books, help others create successful businesses, and more.

Thousands of entrepreneurs, managers, executives, network marketers, and individuals worldwide have applied *The 11th Element* to produce extraordinary results, in less time, with less effort, and a lot more fun—across virtually every industry and niche. For example, by applying the *The 11th Element* system:

- Gary Clark went from being a truck driver to a computer programmer to the CEO of his own company generating sales of $52 million a year.
- Ralf Backstrom launched a successful public relations company in Sweden.
- Bill Harris built his Centerpointe Research Institute business from $12,000 in annual sales to $4.6 million in annual sales.
- Valecia Royer quit a job that was damaging her home life and launched a home-based accounting business that provides her with a strong and steady income, and allows her to spend all the time she wants with her family.
- Bob Serling started a software company from scratch and sold it just 17 months later for $6.2 million—in the middle of a recession!
- Randy Gage went from being a dishwasher in a pancake house to a multimillionaire.

This book also reveals how *The 11th Element* shaped such international success stories as Microsoft, Starbucks, Nike, Reebok, Dell, The Virgin Group and Virgin Atlantic Airways, Kentucky Fried Chicken (KFC), Wendy's restaurants, Marriott, J. K. Rowling's *Harry Potter* phenomenon, Robert Kiyosaki's "Rich Dad, Poor Dad" brand, and more.

People who are plugged in to the kind of raw power supplied by *The 11th Element* are the innovators of the world. They consistently create the breakthroughs and success stories you hear about and see in the news.

It doesn't matter if your interest is in a web-based business, a home-based business, a network marketing business, a small business, a multimillion-dollar business, or a multibillion-dollar business. It doesn't matter if you want to create wealth by trading stocks or bonds, buying and selling real estate, or making other investments. *The 11th Element* can be applied to dramatically improve the results you produce.

Regardless of how effective your promotion, operations, recruiting, distribution, selling system, marketing strategy, or any other aspect of your business might be, *The 11th Element* provides the missing link that pulls it all together in ways you haven't seen yet, acting like a catalyst to create extraordinary success and exponential growth. *The 11th Element* is truly the ultimate tool for creating business success and wealth.

You and I (and everyone else who reads this book) are very different. We have different wants, needs, challenges, and goals. We have unique backgrounds, personalities, environments, and situations. Yet we have one major thing in common—we all have gaps that we must find ways of bridging.

If you're like me and most people I speak with, you're usually clear on what your goals are and what specific results you want to produce. You might want to increase sales and profits, reduce expenses, increase your income, attract and retain top talent, create a new product or service, solve a problem, outfox a competitor, quit your job and replace the income by doing something you enjoy more, or choose a business to start or buy.

What you're not always clear on is what the best way is to get from where you are now to where you really want to be—the best way for you as a unique individual to achieve your goals and produce your results (Figure I.1).

When you know where you are, and you know where you want to go, but you don't know the best way to connect the two locations, a gap is formed that you must find a way to bridge.

At its core, the process of creating successful businesses and wealth consists of bridging a constant stream of gaps. Why? Because

FIGURE I.1 There is a daily challenge on the road to creating business success and wealth.

the minute you bridge one gap to reach a new destination, you'll choose another destination you want to reach, another gap will form, and the process of gap formation and bridging will repeat itself for as long as you continue to desire business success and wealth.

In all the success stories I've personally participated in, I began without knowing how to produce the results I later produced. I began without always having the contacts, ideas, skills, knowledge, and resources I ultimately needed and used to succeed. But I always began with the absolute confidence that I could apply *The 11th Element* system to bridge all the gaps necessary to find what I needed and produce extraordinary results (Figure I.2).

To maximize your results, you need a proven system for bridging your own gaps on a daily basis—for finding the people, ideas, resources, techniques, and strategies you need to produce your own extraordinary results. That's what you'll get from this book.

FIGURE I.2 You need a proven system for bridging the constant stream of gaps that leads to business success and wealth.

By applying the simple "what to do" and "how to do it" secrets you'll discover in this book, you can achieve at levels far beyond what you imagine to be possible—no matter how large or small your goals are.

Like a computer and the Internet, *The 11th Element* is an extremely powerful and versatile tool that can be customized to produce virtually any result. The following applications of the system are only a small sample of what's possible for you:

- *Opportunities:* Find the opportunities (jobs, businesses, investments, partnerships, etc.) that hold the strongest potential for helping you create business success and wealth.

- *Sales and Marketing:* Increase your sales (phone, retail, direct, Internet, mail order, etc.), improve your lead-generating systems, increase your lead-to-sale conversion ratio, dominate your market niche, and leverage your sales and marketing to full advantage.

- *Product Development:* Enhance your existing products or services, and/or add new products and services that can increase your sales and profits.

- *Human Resources:* Attract and keep the top talent (part-time, full-time, or independent contractors) you need to succeed.

- *Finance:* Raise the funding needed to start or grow your business—whether by internal cash flow, bank loan, private investors, a public offering, or other sources.

- *Motivation:* Discover and implement effective strategies for training and motivating employees and sales teams to consistently produce at peak potential.

- *Administrative Issues:* Find the most efficient and cost-effective ways of processing your administrative work—through outsourcing, technology, human resources, or a combination.

- *Morale, Productivity, and Stress Reduction:* Increase job satisfaction, team spirit, and excitement, and reduce the stress associated with rapidly approaching deadlines, not achieving your goals, customers breathing down your neck to produce specific results, or your business going through a difficult time . . . while increasing your levels of enjoyment, focus, and productivity.

The 11th Element is based on core concepts you may not think about much, especially within a business or wealth-building context. It rests on a foundation "the experts" rarely if ever discuss.

Many people who discover *The 11th Element* for the first time instantly recognize the power and potential of the system and are excited to apply and master it. Other people recognize the core concepts and notice they are somehow familiar. These people will tell me, "It's like I've known it all along, but now it has been spotlighted and I see things more clearly."

Still other people experience resistance to the material or skepticism. If you feel such a "negative" reaction coming on, I urge you to carefully monitor and manage it and recognize that the source of your reaction may represent the barrier that has been holding you back from growing your business and wealth to full potential. It's always useful to remember what Albert Einstein said: "If at first the idea is not absurd, then there is no hope for it."[1]

This is why I said that the first of the four steps required to tap into *The 11th Element* is to shift your mind-set. To absorb what you'll discover here, you must approach it with an open mind and be willing to do some serious "outside-the-box" thinking.

Think of this book as if it were a jigsaw puzzle. When you put together a jigsaw puzzle, you dump all the pieces on a table, and at first it doesn't look like much. Then you start putting the pieces together, and slowly but surely, it starts to look like something. Finally, when enough pieces are in place, the "big picture" explodes into view.

You're about to receive a new set of pieces to the puzzle called "how to create business success and wealth." Once you add them to the pieces you've already acquired, a new "picture" will explode into view for you, and you'll be empowered to create success breakthroughs at breakneck speed.

The new puzzle pieces will come in the form of a seven-step process that will be introduced to you in the next chapter—after an important foundation has been laid. The remaining chapters of the book will then describe the seven steps in full detail.

You'll find the new puzzle pieces particularly enlightening if you've tried other "how to build business and wealth" systems but didn't produce the consistent results you wanted. As you'll soon see, there's a lot more to creating business success and wealth than just modeling what others have done, having a strong desire, setting goals, writing a great business plan, having a successful mentor, hiring great people, visualizing, using your subconscious mind, or being persistent.

It is my sincere hope that *The 11th Element* will help you make major changes in your business and life, no matter what you want, or what challenges you're facing right now.

My intent is to plant seeds within you that will continue to germinate and grow long after you read the last page and put this book down. I want to stimulate new thinking in you, and new possibilities for your career, finances, and business.

My intention in writing this book is to open the doorway that connects the visible with the invisible, the seen with the unseen, the known with the mysterious. Albert Einstein also said: "The most beautiful emotion we can experience is the mystical. It is the power of all true art and all science. He to whom this emotion is a stranger, who can no longer wonder and stand rapt in awe, is as good as dead."[2]

Let's open the door, walk through it, and take our first step together toward business success and wealth.

Networking with the Ultimate "Inside Contact"

The world is larger than our view of it.[1]
—Henry David Thoreau

What is essential is invisible to the eye.[2]
—Antoine De Saint-Exupery

The Internet provides an extremely rich metaphor for the concepts I want to introduce in this chapter. To lay the proper foundation, I'll review certain basic Internet concepts with which you may already be familiar. Like millions of people, you've probably used the Internet to:

- Find information and resources
- Share information

- Communicate with other people
- Buy things
- Sell things

The Internet is a tremendous tool. It lets you do new things you couldn't do before, and helps you do old things more quickly and efficiently. To get these benefits, however, you must have Internet access and be able to master certain navigational and surfing skills.

The Internet is nothing more than a network that links millions of computers and allows us to communicate with each other at high speed. By connecting to the Internet and tapping into resources such as web sites, search engines, discussion groups, forums, and e-mail, you can:

- Offer your products and services to a worldwide audience
- Research virtually any subject
- Find a job
- Fill a job opening
- Find and hire freelance professionals to meet virtually every need
- Communicate at lightning speed with anyone—anywhere on the planet
- Share information and documents
- And much, much more

As powerful, amazing, and gigantic as the Internet appears, it is severely limited in its capabilities. There is actually another network you can access to get the help you need to succeed. It's much larger than the Internet, infinitely more powerful, and doesn't require a computer. The mind-set and system for tapping into the other network is *The 11th Element.*

Just as the Internet connects us at the conscious level, this other network connects us at the unconscious level, beneath our conscious level of awareness. The concept of an invisible or unconscious network linking us all together was once considered "new age" or "way out," but scientists all over the world, including those at Harvard University, Stanford Research Institute, and various other private institutions, are now documenting it.

You've tapped into "the invisible network" yourself. Haven't there been times when you knew something was going to happen before it happened? There have been times when you knew who was calling before you picked up the phone, haven't there? Perhaps you had the experience of knowing what someone else was thinking or what they were going to say before they said it. You've had hunches that proved to be accurate, haven't you? Where do you think the knowledge in those situations came from?

Rob Strasser, once a top executive with Nike, felt that the company should invest major resources in the new Nike Air line of shoes, and he pushed the project forward despite tremendous resistance from the Nike management team. Nike Air ended up being one of the most successful product launches Nike ever made. Where do think Strasser got his "feeling"?

In their book *Hard Drive: Bill Gates and the Making of the Microsoft Empire,* James Wallace and Jim Erickson wrote this about Microsoft cofounders Bill Gates and Paul Allen: "Allen, even more than Gates, had a knack for figuring out the direction of the industry three or four years down the road."[3] Where do you think Paul Allen got his "knack"? It had to come from somewhere!

J. Paul Getty, the late oil billionaire and once the world's richest man, and his father both had an uncanny talent for finding oil. Where do you think they got that "talent"?

As you read in the Foreword, several hunches led Robert Allen to build a $100 million business and a vast personal fortune. Where do you think he got his hunches?

Stare at anyone, even through the car window at a stoplight, and he or she will turn to look directly at you. The person "feels" you staring and knows exactly which way to turn his or her head to lock eyes with you. How do you think people know you're looking at them, which direction to turn their heads, and where to focus their eyes?

When I was 16 years old, at 3:00 in the morning, I was in a bad car accident in Milwaukee, Wisconsin, where I grew up. At the exact moment it happened, my mother awoke from a sound sleep, sat straight up in bed, and knew something "bad" had happened to me. How could she possibly have known?

When you meet individuals for the first time and have strong feelings about them (you're attracted to them, you like them, you feel comfortable with them, you feel you can trust them, or you don't like them, you don't feel comfortable with them, or you don't feel you can trust them), what spawns those feelings?

These experiences are examples of how we tap into the invisible network without consciously intending to do so. Everyone has had one or more experiences of tapping into the invisible network. Ask yourself three questions about those experiences:

- *Where* did the information come from?
- *How* did I get it?
- *Why* did I get it?

The real question is not: "Is there really an invisible network connecting us all?" The evidence supporting the existence of such a network is overwhelming. The real question is: "How can I use the invisible network to help me build my business and wealth?" This book answers that question and shows you how—step by simple step.

The invisible network serves two purposes:

1. An information storehouse
2. A communication switchboard

Information Storehouse

On the Internet, huge collections of information are stored in *search engines*. You can use them to research virtually any subject, want, or need. The invisible network has search engines, too, but they're much larger, more complex, and robust in their functionality.

Information about *everything* and *everyone* in the world is automatically sent into the invisible network search engines and stored there. I call this collected information *master biography files.*

For example, if someone is working on a cure for cancer in Japan, developing an invention in Australia, has a special skill and lives in South Africa, offers a unique product or service in the United States, or has new strategies she's applying in England, the details are automatically sent into the master biography files and can be accessed for your benefit. The information in this invisible network is continuously updated on a real-time, moment-to-moment basis as things change worldwide.

This is one of the huge benefits of the invisible network; and why tapping into it helps you bridge those gaps described earlier and provides you with access to raw power that goes far beyond what you're capable of consciously . . . on your own.

Communication Switchboard

People continually send messages into the invisible network (you might think of them as e-mails or newspaper or magazine ads) asking for help to achieve goals and specifying the kind of help they're willing to offer others.

Messages flow through the invisible network at the unconscious level 24 hours a day, 7 days a week. People respond to our messages. We respond to theirs. And just like in the surface world, we discuss, negotiate, make decisions, and make agreements at the unconscious level: "I'll do this for you if you'll do that for me." As a result, something happens on the surface in our lives and businesses.

If you're excited about the Internet, imagine magnifying the available resources and possibilities billions of times. Then you'll have a slight idea of what's possible when you start tapping into the invisible network. You'll discover more of the "why" behind this in later chapters.

It is critical for you to understand that the *primary driving force* behind the results you produce in your business and wealth-building efforts is the flow of information and messages through the invisible network, not what you do in the conscious or surface world you're so familiar with.

No matter what's going in your business or financial life right now—sales, profits, income, operations, employees, net worth, investments, and so on—it's all being shaped in powerful and amazing ways by information and messages that were sent into the invisible network in the past.

Similarly, everything that happens in your business and wealth-building efforts in the future will be shaped in powerful and amazing ways by information and messages that are being sent into the network now and in the future.

You understand how e-mail works. You know that if you send out 20 e-mails with a question, you'll get answers back that you can see and read. You also know that you can't expect answers to questions you never ask. The invisible network works the same way. You must ask for the help you want and need.

It doesn't always look like it on the surface, but at the unconscious level, everyone wants to help others fulfill their life purposes and complete their missions. Just like on the Internet, other people will help you if you ask them properly. You just have to know how to find the right people and how to ask them for help so you get the positive response you desire. (At the unconscious level there is a definite art to this.)

If you want to build your business, increase your sales, maximize your profits, grow your income, create wealth, and improve your quality of life, there are facts and details you absolutely must know about:

- How the invisible network actually works at the unconscious level

- How to send the information and messages you want into the network

- How to receive information and messages through the network
- How to filter and respond to other people's unconscious messages (just like you do with e-mail)
- How the flow of information and messages through the network gets translated into tangible results in your life
- What to do *after* you send information and messages into the network to maximize the benefits you receive

By the time you finish this book, you'll know how to manage and execute each one of these action items.

Although you might not realize it, you can't send an e-mail, receive an e-mail, surf the Web, use search engines, or download files without an Internet Service Provider (ISP) doing a lot of work behind the scenes to help you. It works the same way with access to the invisible network.

It is important to understand this critical fact when working with the invisible network.

Let me repeat: To access the Internet, you need help from someone else who has the equipment, knowledge, and expertise to link you up. It might be AOL or another ISP. *Someone else* must give you access to the Internet. You cannot do it by yourself (unless you have all the equipment and connections of an ISP).

Few people talk about it in a business context, but you have within you an inner intelligence I call your *Inner CEO*. Your Inner CEO is another part of you, a very personal part of *your* mind, *your* consciousness, *your* self, *your* being, whatever you want to call it.

The relationship between you and your Inner CEO is similar to the relationship between a corporate CEO and his executive team. That is, everyone is valued and contributes, but the CEO is in charge and has the ultimate decision-making authority.

Among its other responsibilities, your Inner CEO controls access to the invisible network (like an ISP), and manages the flow of information and messages in and out of the invisible network on your behalf. Your Inner CEO is the keeper of the gate through which all messages and information must pass before going into the invisible network or becoming available to you (see Figure 1.1).

As you'll see by reading the dozens of examples in this book, by doing research, and sending and responding to messages through the invisible network, your Inner CEO can help you generate income streams, create opportunities, find people, build your business, maximize your profits, increase your income, solve problems, create wealth, and improve your quality of life in ways you can't even imagine right now.

FIGURE 1.1   Your Inner CEO controls access to the invisible network and manages the flow of information and messages on your behalf.

Because of a broader perspective and access to the invisible network, your Inner CEO has access to knowledge and resources far beyond those in your conscious awareness. You're never alone on your quest for business success and wealth, even though it often feels that way. Your Inner CEO and the invisible network form a support system you can tap into to share your burden. You receive help every step of the way.

Your Inner CEO works behind the scenes 24 hours a day, 7 days a week, to help you achieve your goals. Unfortunately, it's likely that nobody ever told you:

- That you have an Inner CEO who connects you to the invisible network (like an ISP connects you to the Internet), and participates in managing your business and wealth-building efforts from behind the scenes

- The precise role your Inner CEO plays in your day-to-day life, your business, and your wealth-building efforts

- What your Inner CEO does (and doesn't do) for you, and how he helps you achieve your goals

- How to contact your Inner CEO, communicate directly with him, get answers, ask for help with your projects, and tap into the invisible network

Networking in the outer world is a powerful strategy. Networking in the inner world—through working with your Inner CEO to tap into the invisible network—is a turbocharged strategy, and your Inner CEO is the ultimate inside contact.

Earlier in this, chapter I described the time I was in a bad car accident and my mother woke up out of a sound sleep knowing something bad had happened to me. I also discussed the times when you know who's calling before you pick up the phone, you know what someone is going to say before they say it, or you know that someone is staring at you.

In each of the examples, there's someone sending a message and someone receiving a message through the network. You can call the receiving process intuition, instinct, sixth sense, or whatever you want, but this ability to receive messages through the invisible network is the ultimate power.

To optimize the results you produce on your journey to creating business success and wealth, you must learn how to send and receive information and messages through the invisible network. No matter what results you want, and no matter what you do at the conscious level to produce them, you must supplement your efforts by working with your Inner CEO and sending and receiving messages through the invisible network.

There are people in the world who can help you build your business and create wealth. They're sending messages into the network right now, and information about their activities is stored. Imagine how your world would transform if you could tap into that vast storehouse of information, receive their messages, and hook up with those people to mutual advantage.

No matter what results you want to produce, there are specific techniques, strategies, resources, people, and ideas stored in the invisible network that hold the perfect solution for you and your unique situation. Imagine how your world would transform if you could access those resources and apply their power to support your efforts (see Figure 1.2).

There are times when your Inner CEO wants to send *you* messages in response to messages it sent into the network, or in response to your requests for help. Imagine how your world would transform if you could easily receive messages from your Inner CEO on a consistent basis.

Right now, information and messages in the invisible network are impacting you in major ways. Some of it is helpful to you, and contributes to your efforts in positive ways. Other information and messages may be hurting you, limiting you, and holding you back from fulfilling your true potential.

In addition to learning how to send and receive messages through the network, you absolutely must find out what messages and information are already active, then enhance what's helping

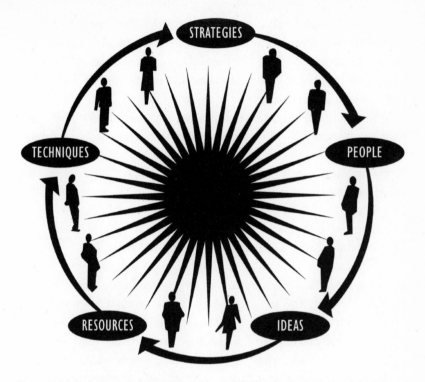

FIGURE 1.2 Business success and wealth are built from people, ideas, resources, techniques, and strategies.

you and change what's holding you back. This book shows you how to do that.

In our daily lives, we keep things secret from other people. We hold things back. Sometimes we have a hard time opening up, getting to know other people, or letting them get to know us. Some people lie about things or distort the truth in other ways. However, in the invisible network, at the unconscious level, there are no secrets.

Because of the way information is stored in the invisible network, your Inner CEO (and everyone else's Inner CEO) has access to complete and unedited information about everyone, and Inner CEOs are constantly communicating with each other as they work to help us from behind the scenes.

When you communicate with other people by e-mail; by phone; in person; by letter, ad, web site, radio, or television, it seems as if they only know what you tell them. But—at the unconscious level where the invisible network operates and where Inner CEOs operate—we're all open books.

Receiving messages through the network from other people (or from your Inner CEO) can help you make better decisions about hiring, product development, marketing, problem solving, strategic direction, and much more. The instructions for how to receive these messages appear in Chapter 6.

Seven Steps That Produce Extraordinary Results

If you want to start or buy a business, information and messages flowing through the invisible network are studied by your Inner CEO to help you make the best choice and get started on the right foot. If you currently have a business, information and messages flowing through the invisible network are shaping your sales and profits, determining who comes into or out of your business (including employees, partners, and customers), what kind of impact they have on you, and the impact you have on them. The information and messages act like magnets, attracting the "right" people and resources and repelling the "wrong" ones.

One phone company's ads told us to "reach out and touch someone" using the telephone system. When tapping into *The 11th Element*, you use the invisible network to "reach out and touch" your Inner CEO, and the people, ideas, resources, techniques, and strategies that can help you most. You do this by taking seven steps. I introduce the steps now and discuss them in detail in later chapters:

1. *Expand and clarify your "ideal outcome."* This process begins with clarifying the specific type of help you want right now, and it continues by expanding your vision to define the lifestyle package in which you would prefer those results to be delivered.

2. *Craft a request for help to produce the optimal outcome.* Once you're clear on the type of help you want and your preferred lifestyle package, you must then make a formal request for help to your Inner CEO. Requesting help is simple, but there are definite guidelines that must be followed to maximize the benefits you receive.

3. *Deliver your request to your Inner CEO for approval.* Once you've crafted your request for help, it must be delivered to your Inner CEO for approval before the next steps can be taken.

4. *Receive approval.* Before your request can be sent into the invisible network to receive responses and before your Inner CEO will begin doing research and due diligence using the invisible network search engines, your request for help must first be approved. Just as in the corporate arena, not all requests or projects will be approved.

5. *Tap into the invisible network for help.* If your request for help is approved, it will be physically sent into the invisible network, much like you would send an e-mail through the Internet. However, Inner CEOs don't need to know who to send the requests to, nor do they have specific e-mail addresses. The invisible network automatically forwards requests for help to the people who can help you most. In addition, your Inner CEO begins to do research using the invisible network search engines and initiates other invisible network activities.

6. *Perform due diligence and make decisions and plans.* After your request is sent into the invisible network, other Inner CEOs will respond, much like you would respond to an advertisement in a magazine or newspaper. Your Inner CEO organizes all the other information and resources gathered during the research step. Discussions will be held; negotiations will be conducted; and decisions, choices, agreements, and action plans will be made.

7. *Manifest the outcome.* After your Inner CEO completes his research, due diligence, negotiations, agreements, and planning

phases, a process is set into motion that results in your desired outcome manifesting in the best possible way, and at the
best possible time.

These seven steps, combined with a proven method by which to
work them, allow you to tap into *The 11th Element* to produce
extraordinary results, in less time, with less effort, and to have a lot
more fun doing it. These seven steps are thoroughly described in
Chapters 4, 5, and 6.

Armed with an understanding of the invisible network and
your Inner CEO, you're now ready to discover the true nature of
the single most powerful force in your life. To make that discovery,
turn to Chapter 2.

The Wild Card Is Always Dealt

Each player must accept the cards life deals him or her. But once they are in hand, he or she alone must decide how to play the cards in order to win the game.[1]

— Voltaire, 1694–1778

Do not follow where the path may lead. Go instead where there is no path and leave a trail.[2]

— George Bernard Shaw

The term *wild card* is used widely in our culture. It generally has two meanings:

1. When referring to card games, it means a playing card that's value can be defined by its holder to suit his purposes at the time. For example, in a game of poker where Jacks are wild,

the player may assign any value to a Jack to improve his hand.

2. When referring to general or slang usage, it means an unpredictable or unforeseeable factor that has major impact. For example, a surprise witness at a trial is often described as the "wild card" that determined the outcome.

There will be wild cards in your business and wealth-building efforts, too, and they will come in the form of unpredictable or unforeseeable events that have major impact on you.

You must now look closely at a truth that's rarely discussed when consulting the experts about creating business success and wealth. The truth is that you came into this life with a specific life purpose or mission. There's something specific you came here to do, contribute, experience, or learn as a result of your time here. Making those contributions, having those experiences, and learning what you came here to learn is your primary "job." It's the journey you came here to take, and it's a very important one. As Richard Bach said, "Here is the test to find whether your mission on earth is finished: If you're alive, it isn't."[3]

Charles Schulz, creator of the comic strip *Peanuts*, said, "It seems beyond the comprehension of people that someone can be born to draw comic strips, but I think I was."[4] Dave Thomas, founder of Wendy's, said, "When I was eight years old, I knew I wanted to be in the restaurant business . . ."[5] Michael Dell and Bill Gates knew from an early age that their "destiny" lay with computers. The examples go on and on.

Not everyone knows what their missions are *consciously* (and conscious knowledge of the mission isn't necessary to succeed as you'll see in later chapters), but your Inner CEO knows all about your mission, and she's responsible for managing all the details to ensure that you complete it. That's *her* job!

The decisions your Inner CEO makes, how she responds to your requests for help, and the way she manages the flow of information and messages through the invisible network are shaped entirely by her knowledge of your mission and purpose, and the big-picture and long-term perspectives it includes. You could think of life purpose and mission as if they were a gigantic filter that all your wants, needs, dreams, and desires must pass through before they become real (see Figure 2.1).

Even though you may not be consciously aware of your life purpose and mission, they exert tremendous influence over what happens and doesn't happen in your life, business, and wealth-building efforts. They're the most powerful forces in your life.

In other words, your business isn't just about sales, profits, personal income, products, services, employees, and building wealth.

FIGURE 2.1 Life purpose and mission filter and shape all the results you produce.

It's also about using the process you go through to build and run your business, and the events, experiences, and benefits that flow out of the process to help you fulfill your life purpose.

Returning to the definitions of wild card, there are two core ideas:

1. A value that's determined by the card player to best suit his or her situation
2. Something unexpected that has major impact

Since our missions are all different, the wild cards we're dealt in our business and wealth-building efforts—and the values we assign to them—will be unique to us. Fill a room with 12 successful people, ask them the secrets to their success, and you'll get 12 different answers. The truth is the world's most successful people create their successes by taking completely different paths, doing completely different things, and applying completely different formulas. There may be similarities on the surface, but when you dig deeper, you see that each story is unique. The why behind that dynamic is different life purposes and missions.

The second definition of wild card—an unforeseeable factor that has major impact—takes three shapes:

1. Events your Inner CEO sets in motion without your awareness (this happens more than you might expect)
2. Events your Inner CEO sets in motion in response to your requests for help
3. Blocks and resistance to your best-laid plans (this too happens more than you might expect and is actually good news, no matter how it may appear)

The path you travel to business success and wealth will, by definition, be unique to you. Everything you experience will be custom designed to help you fulfill your life purpose and complete your mission. You must understand that, accept it, expect it, and plan for it.

As you'll see in later chapters, you always want to be on the lookout for unique solutions versus generic solutions, cookie-cutter solutions, following the crowd, or even the advice of so-called experts.

Your wealth and success will be created through a partnership between you and your Inner CEO, in which your Inner CEO plays the role of senior partner. Events will be set in motion by messages your Inner CEO sends into the network without your conscious awareness (all designed to help you complete your mission), and events will result from the requests you personally send to your Inner CEO that get approved. Many experiences—both good and bad from your perspective—will manifest on your road to success that you won't intend, expect, plan for, or even understand on a conscious level. They will all be managed by your Inner CEO and driven by your mission and purpose.

But the wild card benefits don't stop there. To bridge all the gaps that separate you from where you are now and where you really want to be, and from where you are now and the completion of your mission, you'll need to generate a steady stream of people, ideas, resources, techniques, and strategies. But which people would be best for you and your unique situation? Which ideas? Which resources? Which techniques? Which strategies? How do you choose?

If you do research and perform due diligence to answer those questions by yourself, here's what you'll discover:

- There are many options and they all claim to be the best; this causes tremendous confusion.
- Most of the experts disagree about what the best way is, which makes matters worse.
- You'd never have enough time or energy to apply all the to-do items you compile.

Considering the magnitude of the task, and the fact that your knowledge of your mission and life purpose is limited at best, it's virtually impossible for you to *consciously and effectively* sort through the available options and possible pathways to select the ones best suited to your unique situation and needs. Even if you could do this, it wouldn't be an efficient use of your valuable time.

You need help—everyone does.

You need quick, efficient, and effective ways of filtering all the available options and possible pathways to success so you can zero in with laser-like precision on the people, ideas, resources, techniques, and strategies that are "perfect" for your unique situation, wants, and needs.

How do you do that? By building a relationship with your Inner CEO, and through that relationship, tapping into the tremendous raw power available through the invisible network. You'll learn how to do that in later chapters.

The bottom line is this: It's vital that you understand deep down in your gut that the way your business and wealth-building efforts evolve and unfold will *not* be determined solely by what you *think* you want, or what you see from the limited perspective of your conscious mind. There are larger forces at work, big-picture goals to be achieved, and what you *really want* (to complete your mission in life) to be considered.

Because you need help filtering all the available options and possible pathways to success, and because your Inner CEO can do this on your behalf, it is wise to let go of your conscious mind's desire to control things and allow your Inner CEO to work for you through the invisible network.

When discovering the wild card concept for the first time, people frequently ask, "Does this mean that my entire life is predestined or predetermined and that I have no free will or choice?" Every moment of your life is not predestined or predetermined, although certain big-picture themes, events, relationships, and influences are. I'm a fan of professional football and the Denver Broncos. The Broncos were led to two Super Bowl wins by a fantastic quarterback named John Elway. If you study John Elway's life, it is clear that a big part of his life purpose and mission was to play professional football (the theme), and that many events, relationships, and influences orchestrated by his Inner CEO assisted him in achieving that result. Was every moment of every game determined in advance? No. Was his overall win-loss percentage determined in advance? Absolutely not. Was it predetermined that he'd win two Super Bowls, or that he'd do it in the exact years he did? Again, no.

I believe that a big part of my life purpose and mission is to share *The 11th Element* and my system for tapping into it with a worldwide audience. That kind of big-picture theme was most likely predetermined, but all the details of each day were not planned in advance, or even most of them. What we experience in our daily lives is determined by a process called "on the fly" you'll discover more about in later chapters. The degree to which events and themes are predetermined will be shaped by your life purpose and mission, and this will vary by individual.

When you apply *The 11th Element* and start seeing results, you will begin to fully understand that a strong partnership with your Inner CEO, who knows your mission, sees the big picture, and has access to the invisible network where everybody is an open book is vital to your long-term success.

Now that you understand the true nature of the wild cards that will shape and impact your business and wealth-building efforts, it's time to make one last mind-set shift so you can take full advantage of *The 11th Element* system going forward.

Why the 10 Elements Don't Work

I owe my success to having listened respectfully to the very best advice, and then going away and doing the exact opposite.[1]

—G. K. Chesterton

A s mentioned in the introduction, many books have been written claiming to offer systems for creating business success and wealth. Most discuss or center on a combination of *10 elements* the authors claim are necessary for creating total success. Unfortunately, the discussions of those traditional 10 elements are incomplete, and the systems have high failure rates.

Because so many myths about the first 10 elements are deeply entrenched in the popular culture—and possibly your mind as well—before we can discuss the actual steps you'll take to tap into the power of *The 11th Element*, we must blow the roof off those myths and set the record straight so you can start your journey with a fresh, clean, and truly empowering mind-set.

To create business success and wealth by tapping into *The 11th Element*, two things must happen:

1. Your requests for help must be approved and sent into the invisible network.
2. Your Inner CEO must tap into the invisible network to search for the best people, ideas, resources, techniques, and strategies to help you.

Therefore, when choosing a business success and wealth-creation strategy, the key question to ask yourself is: "Is this the *best* strategy for getting my requests sent into the network and for getting my Inner CEO to tap into the invisible network to help me with my projects?"

Keeping that question in mind and recalling what you now know about the invisible network, your Inner CEO, and how your life purpose and mission are used as a filter for what happens and doesn't happen in your life, we take a close look at the 10 traditional success elements.

Element 1: Desire

The experts say that you must have a burning desire for wealth and success or you won't create it. Desire can be a very important element, but for every example of someone who had a burning desire to produce a result and produced it, you'll find countless examples of other people who had absolutely no desire and produced the same result anyway.

J. K. Rowling is a perfect example. Rowling, author of the wildly successful *Harry Potter* books and movies, embodies one of the most incredible success stories of all time. Rowling wanted to earn just enough money to satisfy her desire to write. That's it. We'll get more into her story later, but for now, it's important to see that she had absolutely no conscious desire to produce the kind of monetary success she did. And yet, she's now one of the world's wealthiest people and on the road to becoming the first billionaire author.

Dave Thomas, founder of the Wendy's chain, didn't have a conscious desire to build a restaurant chain or amass a large personal fortune. He just loved the restaurant business and wanted to have "three or four restaurants in the Columbus, Ohio, area."[2]

Blue Ocean Software is one of the biggest success stories I've personally been part of. When Blue Ocean CEO Russ Hobbs and I first started working together, we had absolutely no conscious desire for the company to evolve the way it did or to create as much wealth for as many people as we did.

Warren Buffett didn't consciously desire to become a multibillionaire or one of the world's richest men when he first entered the field of investing. Neither did the late Sam Walton when he founded Wal-Mart.

In my seminars, talks, and private consulting sessions, I'm often asked about this phenomenon. People say, "Why do some people become so successful without wanting or intending it?" I always answer the same way: "Because producing the result we call success was part of their life purpose and mission, and their Inner CEO was working aggressively to help them from behind the scenes without their awareness. It happens all the time."

On the flip side of this dynamic, there are countless people who had a clear, burning desire to succeed or produce specific results, but their businesses failed despite it. Perhaps that has even happened to you.

If desire was actually necessary, none of these stories would be possible. If you look closely at the lives of wealthy and successful people, you see that while the desire is often present, it isn't a requirement and it isn't necessary. To have impact, desire must be in alignment with your life purpose and mission.

Element 2: Belief

"Whatever you believe becomes your reality," the experts say. In other words, you have to believe you can create a successful business and wealth, or you won't. If you look closely, you'll see people with negative or limiting beliefs who consistently succeed despite those beliefs, and you'll see people with positive or empowering beliefs who consistently fail to produce such results.

There are thousands of examples of people who built enormously successful businesses and fortunes and had tremendous self-doubt and a lack of confidence in the core idea that made them wealthy.

Again, the example of J. K. Rowling stands out. Rowling had tremendous self-doubt and almost abandoned the *Harry Potter* project numerous times. In fact, at one point, she allowed her sister to read part of the manuscript, and she said that if her sister hadn't liked it, she would have dropped the whole thing because she had no confidence in the value of the book. Yet her books are among the best-selling books of all time.

If you could have seen all the doubts and negative beliefs swirling through my head about the projects I've been involved in during my career, you wouldn't have believed I could possibly create the wealth and success I created.

Yet I've done it—over and over.

Similarly, during my seven-year bout with Murphy's Law, the opposite was also true. I believed I would continue to succeed before my crash began, and yet the crash started anyway. After my bad luck continued for a while, I believed it was just a temporary blip and I'd soon return to my successful ways—yet the crash continued for seven long and painful years.

A belief—whether positive or negative—isn't powerful enough to produce results on its own. Like desire, a belief must be in alignment with your life purpose and mission if it's going to have impact.

Remember, all the results you produce in your life are driven by information and messages flowing through the invisible network—and your Inner CEO manages and controls that flow. If you have negative or limiting beliefs about producing specific results and those results aren't in alignment with your life purpose and mission, your beliefs can be disabled by your Inner CEO and not allowed to have impact.

Similarly, if you have positive or empowering beliefs about producing specific results and those results aren't in alignment with your mission or life purpose either, your beliefs can also be disabled by your Inner CEO and not allowed to have impact.

Finally, if your Inner CEO is working on projects independent of your conscious awareness and the completion of those projects is part of your life purpose and mission, what you believe about them will have absolutely no impact at all.

Similar to desire, belief is often present, but it isn't a requirement for success.

Element 3: The Law of Attraction (or You Get What You Expect)

The law of attraction guarantees that you invariably attract into your life people and situations in harmony with your dominant thoughts. Like desire and belief, however, we all have plenty of *dominant thoughts* and *expectations* (positive and negative) that aren't attracted into our lives.

If you look at your own life, you'll see many situations where you had dominant thoughts about something wonderful happening, and yet it didn't. Similarly, there have been times in your life when you had dominant thoughts about something bad happening, and yet it didn't happen either. This concept is positioned as the "law" of attraction, and if it's a law, it must work every time. Yet, the evidence shows that it doesn't work every time.

I'm working on healing and releasing the core causes of this, but I can tell you that there's seldom a public speaking engagement or radio or television interview I do where I don't have dominant thoughts about going blank when it's time to speak or answer a question, about making a fool of myself, or about people hating what I say. Yet none of these things has ever happened. Not even once.

As you're beginning to see, each of these popularized elements of success has significant problems. These problems arise from our Inner CEOs working on projects independent of what we can see with our conscious minds and our Inner CEOs using our missions and life purposes as filters to determine what does and doesn't happen in our lives.

Element 4: Goal Setting

"Set clear goals, review them every day, and you'll succeed" is the familiar cry, yet the failure rate for goal setting is extremely high.

Setting goals is important because it helps you get clear on what you think you want, and the clearer you are, the easier it is to craft requests for help to your Inner CEO. But other than making the process of asking for help easier, there isn't anything magical or turbocharged about goal setting as a strategy.

In fact, when you set a goal, at best, all you're doing is putting a request for help to produce a specific outcome onto the metaphorical desk of your Inner CEO. As a result, the process of reviewing your goals every day isn't necessary or valuable. Once your Inner CEO gets the request, *if* he gets it, he has it, and repetition isn't necessary. It's the equivalent of asking an assistant to go to the office supply store to buy copy paper, then as they're leaving to perform the errand, pulling them back and asking them again to get the copy paper, and then repeating the process indefinitely. Your assistant got the message the first time, is working on it, and doesn't need a reminder.

Finally, goals are simply a statement of what you *think* you want from the limited perspective of your conscious mind, and they can be heavily influenced by friends, associates, loved ones, the media, and others to get you focused in directions that have nothing to do with your true life purpose and mission. As a result, most goals aren't achieved—either at all or exactly as defined—even for the world's most successful people.

Element 5: Modeling

"If you want to produce a result," the experts tell you, "go find someone else who did what you want to do, do what they did, and you'll succeed, too." The idea is that modeling offers a shortcut to success. Again, however, we see an incomplete and flawed strategy.

First, if you look closely, it's almost impossible to find out what somebody else *really* did on their road to wealth and success. In so many cases, successful people don't know or remember exactly what they did. In addition, many times, even if they do know and remember, they won't tell you the complete story because they're afraid they'd somehow lose out (to competitors present or future) if they revealed all their secrets.

Second, even if they know exactly what they *think* they did to succeed and they're willing to tell you, they can't tell you what information or messages in the invisible network impacted their success or what their Inner CEOs did from behind the scenes to help them.

Third, even if you could duplicate the exact steps someone else took, you wouldn't want to. Why? Because people are unique. They have unique life purposes, unique missions, and unique Inner CEOs that, for years, have been sending unique requests into the invisible network and doing research to find unique solutions to help them carve out unique paths to success.

The odds are strong that even if you tried to duplicate what someone else did exactly, it wouldn't work for you. The strategy you tried to copy would need to be tweaked, refined, revised, and changed to match *your* mission and life purpose and to create true success for you.

While learning from others can be valuable, you ultimately should concentrate on carving out unique paths as you'll discover in greater detail in the next chapter. As you apply *The 11th Element* system, your focus should be on asking your Inner CEO for help to find personalized, customized, unique solutions. That's where the real power is. Working with your Inner CEO and the invisible network is the ultimate shortcut, not copying what others have done.

When asked "How can I make a million dollars," J. Paul Getty, the late billionaire oil tycoon, said in his book *How to Be Rich*, "I can't give you any sure-fire formulas, but I'm certain of one thing. You'll go much further if you stop trying to look and act and think like everyone else on Madison Avenue or Wacker Drive or Wilshire Boulevard. Try being a nonconformist for a change. Be an individualist—and an individual. You'll be amazed at how much faster you'll 'get ahead'."[3]

Getty continued, "In my opinion, no one can possibly achieve any real and lasting success or 'get rich' in business by being a conformist. A businessman who wants to be successful cannot afford to imitate others or to squeeze his thoughts and actions into trite and shopworn molds. He must be very much of an individualist who can think and act independently. He must be an original, imaginative, resourceful and entirely self-reliant entrepreneur. If I may be permitted the analogy, he must be a creative artist rather than merely an artisan of business."[4]

How do you ensure that you become an original, imaginative, resourceful, and entirely self-reliant entrepreneur? By working with your Inner CEO and tapping into the invisible network.

Getty continued, "The successful businessman's nonconformity is most generally—and most obviously—evident in the manner and methods of his business operations and activities. These will be unorthodox in the sense that they are radically unlike those of his hidebound less imaginative—and less successful—associates or competitors."[5]

Michael Dell agreed with this approach when he wrote, "We learned the importance of ignoring conventional wisdom and doing things our way."[6]

I'm not saying there's no value in modeling or learning from the success of others. Many times, after tapping into the invisible network, your Inner CEO will lead you to a mentor who will offer tremendous value to you. But you must have a clear and objective perspective about applying modeling as a strategy. I have never modeled successful people and done exactly what they did, but I have studied successful people, looked at what they did, then worked with my Inner CEO to pick and choose specific pieces of their strategies, or to refine these strategies and make them my own. This is the kind of mind-set you want to have.

Element 6: Create a Clear and Detailed Plan

"You need to create a clear and detailed plan for carrying out your desire" is what most experts will tell you. Plans are definitely important. Successful businesses and wealth can't be created without a plan existing somewhere. But the key question to ask yourself is: Who should be doing the planning?

Here's the problem: You and I don't know the details of our life purposes and missions. We don't know what projects our Inner CEOs have in the works right now or which new ones they plan to launch in the near future. We have limited knowledge of the information and messages flowing through the invisible network at any given moment—about us, our projects, or the other people, ideas, resources, techniques, and strategies that could help us. No matter how skilled or intelligent we may be, we simply can't keep up with the complex, fast-moving, and rapidly changing world we live in.

As a result, there is often a *huge* difference between what we *think* we want, from the limited perspective of our conscious minds, and what we *really* want, from the big-picture perspective of our Inner CEOs, our missions, and our life purposes.

For example, in the final two years of my work with Blue Ocean Software, the management team was focused on launching an initial public offering (IPO). We had everything ready to go, and because of the amazing growth and profitability results we produced, the investment bankers considered us the first-round draft choice for the upcoming IPO season. Our clear and detailed plan was to go public in the first quarter of 2003.

However, the entire plan changed when the IPO market for technology companies dried up unexpectedly and showed no signs of strengthening in the near future. When software giant Intuit came courting, we ended up selling the company for $177 million instead.

Was there anything wrong with the fact that we had a plan? No. Was there anything wrong with the specific plan we had? No, not at all. Was there anything wrong with our guiding our actions by that plan? Again, no. But it's important to understand that many of the plans we make—at the conscious level—don't have staying power or validity because they're based on our very limited perspectives.

In the Blue Ocean example, like so many others you will encounter along your road to wealth and success, limited perspective and "wildcards" can cause even the best-laid plans to fall by the wayside.

I have plans right now that take me six to eight months into the future, and that's it. Even in such a short time frame, it's likely that some or all of my plans will be revised or dropped. While I have ideas, preferences, and feelings about what's ahead of me, I don't have 3-year plans, 5-year plans, or 10-year plans. Why? Because I look forward and say to myself, "What's the point? I have no idea who I'm going to be at that point in time, what I'll want or need. I have no idea what kinds of opportunities are going to come my way between now and then. I have no idea about all the other projects my Inner CEO is or will be working on independently of me. What's the point of my creating such long-term plans when the odds are they're going to change dramatically?"

Am I saying not to have or use plans? No. I'm saying that plans have a greater chance of success if they come from the combined efforts of you and your Inner CEO and if they can be created, managed, and updated based on information coming through the invisible network.

I'm also saying that you'll be better served if you carve your plans out of clay versus stone so they can be easily reshaped as necessary. We'll discuss this idea in more detail in later chapters.

Element 7: Take Massive Action Now!

The concept of *taking massive action* has become popular in the self-help and success literature. Start this minute. Then do something every day to help you achieve your goals. Action, action, action. That's the key.

I'm a very proactive, action-oriented person. But I've learned that sometimes *now* is the *right* time to take action, and sometimes now is the *wrong* time to take action—whether it's massive or minimal.

The birth of this book is a perfect example. I wanted this book to be published by a major New York publisher. To achieve that goal, I decided I needed to have a literary agent. So I focused my conscious attention and used *The 11th Element* system to get myself an agent. Associates introduced me to agents, but no one was interested. I did research on my own and sent book proposal packages to dozens of top agents, but no one was interested.

Every time a round of agent solicitation "failed," however, I sent a request to my Inner CEO for help, and I noticed that something would happen to cause me to redo the concept of the book and the proposal package. The examples changed, the chapter titles and organization changed, the buzzwords I used to describe my concepts changed, and so on. Some things changed just because I went back to the drawing board, and other things changed because I had new experiences and new insights into how to best communicate the material I'd been using with such success.

I'd emerge from each revision with renewed confidence and optimism, but for two years the doors to major New York publishers remained closed to me. It didn't matter if best-selling authors gave me introductions to their agents or editors and implored them to take me on as a client. Everything I did "failed."

I kept evolving the project based on the guidance I was receiving from my Inner CEO. I kept sending out proposal packages and following up on leads. One day, after sending out four freshly revised proposal packages to top agents, two called and wanted to represent me—including one who had turned me down two times in the past.

I chose one of the agents, Michael Broussard, and two weeks later, he sent out nine packages to contacts he had at major New York publishers. Michael sent the packages on a Tuesday afternoon by Airborne Express for delivery Wednesday by 11:00 A.M. Wednesday afternoon at 2:00 P.M., Michael got a call from Airié Stuart, an editor at John Wiley & Sons. As soon as this editor read the proposal, she said, "I want this book. I'm excited by this!" We received strong interest from other publishers, too, but we decided to sign a contract with John Wiley & Sons.

Why did everything flow so quickly, easily, and smoothly with Michael and Airié after all the resistance and "failure" during the preceding two years? Because this time it was the right book, the right time, the right agent, the right editor, and most importantly, there was complete alignment with my mission and life purpose. The ease came because of a plan my Inner CEO had been working on all this time.

I believe the book project unfolded in the most perfect way for me. And yet, from my current perspective on *The 11th Element* (despite my success and familiarity with the system, I'm constantly evolving it and gaining new insights), I believe it might have been possible for me (and might be possible for you one day) to have produced the same result with a lot less effort and frustration if I'd been more patient, taken less action, and waited for a clear signal that said, "Now: Go for it *now*!" You'll discover how to ask for and get signals like that in later chapters.

"Timing is everything" is a popular and truthful description of how the world really works. To maximize the benefits received, you want to take massive action only when it's the best time to act, and knowledge of what the best time is can come only from your Inner CEO and access to information in the invisible network.

Element 8: Persistence

"Be persistent, never give up, and you'll succeed." Ever heard that before? Unfortunately, persistence is also an incomplete and flawed strategy.

If you study the lives of wealthy and successful people, you'll find many examples of people who persevered through tremendous resistance and rejection, until they finally had their breakthrough. Persistence *can* lead to success.

However, for every example of persistence leading to success, there are thousands of examples of persistence leading to disaster. Persistence is a valuable strategy when you're being persistent about something that's aligned with your mission and your life purpose— and the timing is right.

Persistence is a strategy that should be applied with great caution and care, however, and not positioned as a law, rule, or formula to be applied by everyone in every situation. You want to be *appropriately persistent,* which means being persistent when you're in alignment with your life purpose and your mission, and backing off or slowing down when you're not. To borrow a phrase from the game of poker, you must know when to *hold* (keep going) and when to *fold* (back off and go in another direction).

When I share this concept with clients and associates, they often ask me, "Well, how do you know when and how to be *appropriately persistent?*" That's something you must work out with your Inner CEO: Use *The 11th Element* system to ask for help, guidance, or a sign. We discuss how to do that in the following chapters.

Element 9: Visualization

"Consistently visualize what you want, and you'll get it." Unfortunately, like the previous eight elements, visualization has an extremely high failure rate. There are three primary reasons for this:

1. It's very difficult to translate the richness of detail that's possible with *The 11th Element* system into a picture. The more detailed, specific, and rich your requests for help are, the greater the likelihood that they will manifest as you intend them to. Therefore, if every picture you create in your imagination has limited *communication ability*, you sacrifice power each time you construct one.

2. There is a saying, "A picture is worth a thousand words." This also means that pictures are subject to interpretation; thus, what you intended to communicate with your picture and what your Inner CEO gets may be worlds apart. Therefore, if your visualization does end up on the desk of your Inner CEO as a request for help—and many do not—the translated request might not be for what you really wanted.

3. The results you want to produce may not be in alignment with your mission and life purpose; therefore, your visualized requests for help may not get approved, even if your picture gets onto the desk of your Inner CEO and it clearly communicates your intent.

Visualization is simply one possible way of getting a request for help onto the desk of your Inner CEO. There's nothing inherently powerful about the act of visualizing. It doesn't guarantee that your request will be approved, go into the invisible network, or become manifest. As you'll soon see, there are far more effective ways of getting your requests for help onto the desk of your Inner CEO.

Element 10: Affirmations

The experts tell you, "Write or speak a clear, present-tense description of your goal as you'd like to see it. Repeat the process often, and you will get what you affirm."

They suggest using phrases such as "I am earning $10,000 a month," or "I always X," or "I consistently draw Y into my life." The experts give you many rules and formulas for how the affirmation needs to be constructed to produce results. Yet, like goal-setting and visualization, the failure rate for affirmations is extremely high.

Affirmations can be a very powerful technique for reprogramming your unconscious mind and changing beliefs. They have value there. But they are an extremely inefficient way of getting a request for help on the desk of your Inner CEO.

Look at it this way: Your Inner CEO monitors everything you're saying to yourself, everything you're thinking, and everything that happens to you on a daily basis. Imagine that he hears you saying to yourself, "I effortlessly earn $10,000 a month every month of the year" or some such phrase. Is that a request for help? Does that motivate him to tap into the invisible network to help you produce that result? Possibly, but at best, it's a weak strategy for getting the help you want.

In my work with clients, I often say, "Don't make statements. Ask for help."

In addition, affirmations are usually so short that, like visualization, they don't have the kind of richness of detail that really gives you the power you're looking for and that's available by working with your Inner CEO in other ways.

Do you see how many missing links the traditional 10 elements have and how much additional power is available to you when you tap into *The 11th Element?* Do you see that the assumption flowing through all 10 traditional elements is that you have the ability, through the various techniques, to tap into the invisible network directly to produce results?

Always remember this: No matter what you're doing, no matter what you want help with, no matter what technique you're using, everything starts with a request for help that goes to the desk of your Inner CEO. If the request is approved, invisible network activity is initiated and your desired outcome will manifest. But everything goes to the desk of your Inner CEO first. Nothing goes directly into the network without first being evaluated to see how it fits in with your mission and life purpose, the projects currently being worked on, and the projects that are scheduled to launch soon. There is always a filter.

Having a filter like that is a tremendous gift. When you really "get in your gut" that such a filter is operational, you can relax more deeply into your process and stop worrying about making mistakes. A filter keeps unwanted outcomes from manifesting in your world and helps you complete your mission in the best way and with the best timing.

Now that you've got a fresh, clean, and truly empowering mind-set, we can take the next step to discover how to craft the best possible requests for help.

The Rules of the Game

There is only one success—to be able to live your life in your own way.[1]

—Christopher Morley

A s discussed in Chapters 2 and 3, your business and wealth-building efforts will be shaped by a partnership between you and your Inner CEO, in which your Inner CEO acts as senior partner. When you want help with a project, there are rules of the game and a specific process to follow to maximize your odds of success. The first two steps in that system are discussed in this chapter:

Step 1: Expand and clarify your ideal outcome.

Step 2: Craft a request for help to produce the optimal outcome.

Step 1: Expand and Clarify Your Ideal Outcome

Expanding and clarifying your ideal outcome begins by simply assessing the type of help you need at any given moment and then prioritizing. Do you want help to increase sales, reduce expenses, improve your marketing, fill a job opening, improve the productivity of your employees, or expand your product line? Is there a problem that needs to be solved? Are you looking for new investment opportunities or ways to increase the profitability of your stock or commodity trading? Do you want to build your downline larger or faster? Is there a specific resource you need to find? Scan your world and note any areas where you need help or that could use improvement.

When you first begin applying *The 11th Element* system, list all the projects, tasks, results, and outcomes with which you want help. If you have numerous requests on your list, prioritize them by importance and potential impact on your affairs. Ask yourself, "If I could get help with all my projects, tasks, results, and outcomes, which ones would have the most impact on my business, finances, and quality of life?" Then reorder the items on your list and craft requests for each one by priority.

When you're first using *The 11th Element* system, you'll probably have a long list of requests, so prioritizing is very important. As you continue using the system and working through your backlog, your focus will shift to a present-moment "What's up right now; what needs attention right now; what do I need help with right now?"

The process of clarifying your ideal outcome then involves expanding your vision of what you want help with to define and ask for the *preferred lifestyle package* in which you want the help delivered. Most people focus on producing specific results but don't consider the lifestyle implications involved with producing them. By taking this step, you can have tremendous positive impact on your quality of life, happiness, stress level, and relationships.

Results can be delivered in virtually any lifestyle package, and you must carefully consider and then specify your preference. I call this the *Lifestyle Imperative*. For example, many people I work with want to earn $250,000 a year or become millionaires. Those goals can be achieved by working 20 hours a day or 2 hours a day. They can be achieved with hundreds of employees or no employees. They can be achieved while working for yourself or for someone else. They can be achieved in a fast-paced, high-stress environment, or a relaxed and laid-back one. They can be achieved while having a great deal of time to spend with your loved ones or very little. They can be achieved with much traveling or very little.

Are there certain hours you'd prefer to work and not work? What would you prefer to do or not do in those hours? Are there certain tasks you love to work on, that you're really good at, and are there other tasks you dislike and would love to offload to someone else? What kind of people do you want to work with? What kind of personality would you prefer in a boss, associate, prospect, customer, or partner?

The lifestyle package possibilities are virtually limitless. Determine which components matter most to you, and state them as your preference in each request for help, as appropriate. You may not always get the exact lifestyle package you ask for, but if you ask, the worst thing that can happen is you have a small amount of frustration or disappointment to manage. The best thing that can happen is you get exactly what you asked for or something similar. If you don't ask, you lose the opportunity, unless you're lucky and your Inner CEO was working on it independently.

For example, I have an extremely successful Internet-based business that sells a variety of products and services. It generates a huge and still growing income for me within a lifestyle package that suits me very well.

I was able to build that business within my preferred lifestyle package because from day one, I made the complete package a priority. On a daily basis, as the seeds I initially planted for the business began to grow, I became more and more clear on what I wanted to do, what I didn't want to do, how I wanted my days to flow, and so on. I then used *The 11th Element* system to ask for help to create that package. I didn't get the whole package immediately.

It actually took three years for all the pieces to fall into place, but now I have it. The key is that I was asking for it from day one, which is what I want you to do as well.

All your requests for help won't have lifestyle packages associated with them, but when they do, it's very important to carefully consider your preferences, get as clear as you can on what you want, and ask for help to have the outcomes delivered within those packages. In many cases, things look very different when you actually reach a destination than they looked when you imagined what the destination would look like before you got there. Therefore, if your wants, needs, or lifestyle packages change at a later date, you can always go back, redefine the package you requested, and ask your Inner CEO for help to make changes.

Now that you've listed the projects, tasks, results, and outcomes you want help with and the lifestyle packages associated with them (I call this your *raw material*), you're ready to move on to the next step—actually crafting your requests for help.

Step 2: Craft a Request for Help to Produce the Optimal Outcome

To craft a request for help that has the greatest likelihood of being approved, going into the invisible network, and having your ideal outcome become manifest, apply all 11 guidelines that I use in my daily life and with clients and students. At the end of the chapter, I provide examples of actual requests that incorporate the guidelines so you can see how to combine them.

Guideline 1: Remember That You're Making Only a Request

It's very important to start the request-drafting process by understanding that your requests are only requests, and they may or may not be approved by your Inner CEO. They are only what you think you want from the limited perspective of your conscious mind.

Once you get your request onto the desk of your Inner CEO for approval, it will be carefully considered. Your Inner CEO will consider the impact it might have on other projects currently underway and on other projects that are ready to be launched. The impact it might have on your life purpose and mission will also be considered. Many other variables will be considered; then, a decision will be made as to whether it ought to manifest and, if so, how and when.

If you've worked in a corporate environment, this should sound familiar because you've had numerous projects you wanted greenlighted or funded. You asked for approval from a boss, partner, board of directors, banker, or investor. Sometimes you got the green light and the funding. Sometimes you didn't. Sometimes you got everything you wanted, sometimes just part. It works the same way with requests sent to your Inner CEO.

Just like the corporate environment, when working with your Inner CEO, you want to ask for what you want and passionately advocate for it, but you want to avoid getting emotionally invested in particular outcomes manifesting at all, within specified time frames, or looking specific ways.

When working with *The 11th Element,* if you get emotionally invested and/or stubbornly keep trying to go down a path that isn't in your best interest, you set yourself up for pain and make it more difficult for your Inner CEO to help you. That's why I spent so much time talking about wild cards in Chapter 2, about the fact that you're not driving the bus, and that what you think would be best for you is only what your conscious mind thinks would be best for you and is often incorrect.

Despite the success I've been able to create in business and my own finances and my familiarity with *The 11th Element* system, I'm wrong time and time again about what I think would be best for me. I frequently have preferences. I'm often absolutely certain something would be fantastic for me or that something that's happening is bad for me. And I often find out I was dead wrong. In each case, the reason for my drawing the incorrect conclusion was the limited perspective of my conscious mind.

Beginning the process of drafting your requests with this attitude also creates a strong sense of humility, which will be invaluable for your long-term success and your emotional well-being. Not being emotionally invested in or attached to specific outcomes gives you more flexibility, more options, and more power. You can also reduce stress in your life by not being invested and being able to go with the flow a bit more. We discuss this in greater detail in later chapters.

This is one of the most difficult mind-set adjustments for many people to make when they first start applying *The 11th Element* system. We've all been programmed so strongly to believe that we're driving the bus, that we're in control, and that we really know what's best for us; such beliefs can be tough to let go of. I promise you, however, that if you can take that leap—jump that gap—and really get that your Inner CEO is in charge, it will serve you well for the rest of your life.

Guideline 2: Ask for Help with All Your Tasks and Projects

Before you perform any important task or begin any project in your business or wealth-building efforts (attend a meeting, make a sales call, attend a seminar, start an interview with a candidate for a job opening, begin working with a new vendor, take on a new client, and so forth), always ask for help in producing the outcome you prefer.

Ultimately, you're going to establish a rhythm with your Inner CEO, and you'll discover that there are certain things you don't have to ask for because they're already being handled. In the beginning, however, I suggest that ask for help every time you have an important task or project. It's important to get your feet wet with the art of crafting requests, with mastering the skills, seeing what happens afterward, reacting to what happens, and building a relationship with your Inner CEO.

I currently have 60 open requests for help. That's slightly high for me, but at any given moment, I have numerous open requests because I'm asking for help with everything I consider important. I suggest that you do the same. You also don't have to limit your requests to business or wealth-building activities either, although that's the primary purpose for this book. You can ask for help with personal issues, too. Here are some examples of the types of requests for help I submitted to my Inner CEO over the last 12 months:

- Help with our move from Florida to Virginia
- Resolve a dispute with another company without legal action
- Help make my wife's delivery of our son be as healthy, comfortable, and pain-free as possible for both of them
- Help my infant son sleep through the night
- Help resolve an emotional issue that was stimulating anger in me
- Help me find a new web-hosting company for my Internet business
- Help write and edit the proposal for this book
- Help find the perfect house in Charlottesville, Virginia and to buy it for the best possible price at the best possible time for our move
- Help with the creation and marketing of a new home-study course I was developing
- Help design and launch my Ultimate Lifestyle Academy
- Help increase the sales of my first book, *The Invisible Path to Success*
- Help guide the contractors doing the remodels of our new home to do the work properly, on time, and within budget
- Help guide the copywriter I hired to create the ad and sales letter I requested
- Help for me and my attorney in negotiating several contracts

- Help have as much positive impact and profitability as possible from a teleseminar I conducted
- Help keep my wife strong and centered when she was sleep deprived after the birth of our son
- Help guide my personal trainer to help me accomplish my physical fitness goals
- Help resolve a digestive issue I was struggling with

My friend Ava told me about an ancient saying, which I absolutely love: "Trust in Allah and tie your camel." You never know what projects your Inner CEO is working on from behind the scenes. You don't want to assume anything, and you want to make sure all your bases are covered, so a wise strategy is to ask for help with everything.

Why is tying your camel in this way so important? Because if you ask for help, you make sure your Inner CEO knows what you want, and you create the possibility for activity to be initiated in the invisible network because that's where the magic happens. If you don't ask for help and your Inner CEO wasn't already working on producing your ideal outcome, no request can go into the network, no research will be done in the invisible network search engines, and nothing will move in your world.

If you're confused about something, send a request to your Inner CEO asking for clarity or the kind of guidance you want. If you need help finding the perfect products or services to sell in your business or the best strategies or techniques for selling them, ask for help. If you need help to find the best business to start or buy, ask for help. If you need to find the perfect employee, contractor, or vendor, ask for help. If you need help solving problems or getting along better with a boss, employee, or associate, ask for help. If you find yourself feeling afraid, worried, or angry about something and you don't want to feel that way any more, send a request for relief and healing to your Inner CEO.

It doesn't matter what specific outcome you want to produce. There's no such thing as a small, unimportant, or invalid request.

Your Inner CEO treats all requests as important when she is looking at them.

You don't want to work with one hand tied behind your back. Ask for help with everything that's up, everything that's having impact on you, or that could have impact if it moved or changed.

Guideline 3: As Appropriate, Divide Your Desired Outcome into Pieces and Ask for Help with Each Piece

Larger and more complex outcomes can be divided into smaller pieces, and when appropriate, it's important to divide them up and ask for help with each piece within the same request. At other times, a simple and general request is fine.

An example of this relates to the proposed Blue Ocean Software IPO. An IPO is a complicated undertaking. I could have simply crafted a request that said "Help us have a successful IPO," but that's too general. There were specific steps along the way where we knew we needed help.

We wanted to align with a top-tier venture capital firm to help open doors to the best investment bankers. We wanted to get at least two heavy hitters from the software industry to join our board of directors for a credibility boost. We wanted to create a strong buzz about the company in the financial community so investors would want to buy the stock when the IPO launched. We wanted to align with a top-tier investment banker to actually launch the IPO. We wanted to generate a strong initial stock price so the company would have the highest possible valuation. We wanted to choose the best timing to do all of this. And we wanted to thoroughly enjoy the wild ride of doing an IPO. So I crafted a request that divided the goal of having a successful IPO into those specific pieces, and I asked for help with each piece. An example of the request I wrote appears at the end of this chapter.

How do you know if, when, and how to divide your requests into pieces? Sometimes you'll just know because it's obvious. At other times, you'll need to invest additional time to ask yourself, "Am I being too general? Are there subsets to this request?" If in doubt, divide it into pieces. As long as you follow the guidelines in this book, you can rarely go wrong by being too specific, but you can sacrifice power by being too general.

In addition, I'm often asked if multiple requests for *separate outcomes* should be combined into one master request or divided into separate requests. There is no hard-and-fast rule for this. I tend to craft separate requests or group them together by theme. For example, I might craft one long request about multiple related financial issues, with finances being the common theme, but I rarely combine separate themes into one request (such as finances and relationships). This is really up to you, and you will need to see what works best for you and your Inner CEO. When in doubt on such questions, simply bring it back to the corporate arena and do your best to answer them. For example, in this case, ask yourself, "Would a corporate CEO prefer getting one 250-page proposal requesting approval on 25 unrelated projects simultaneously or 25 tightly focused proposals grouped by theme and presented individually?" Most of the CEOs I've worked with prefer receiving tightly focused proposals because they're easier to read, easier to focus on and make decisions about, but different people (and Inner CEOs) have different preferences, and you must see what works best for you.

There is a definite art to deciding when to divide requests into pieces, which pieces, and how to divide them, which you'll master over time. It just takes some time and practice. The request examples at the end of this chapter will help you, and additional resources are available at my web sites http://www.11thelement.com and http://www.ultimatelifestyleacademy.com.

Guideline 4: Be Precise about What You Want, but Leave the Response Options Open-Ended

All messages sent through the invisible network are taken literally by everyone reading them—including your Inner CEO. No one second-guesses you. No one tries to read between the lines. No one tries to figure out what you mean.

The invisible network works on an exact-match system, so you must be extremely precise in defining the specific type of help you want. Approach your request crafting with the belief that words mean nothing unless precisely defined. When I'm working with new students and clients to help them craft their requests, I frequently see wording such as:

- "Big profits"
- "Fast"
- "Increase my income"
- "Improve my relationship"
- "Have more time with my family"
- "Resolve my money concerns"
- "Get fantastic results"

In such cases, I usually reply by saying:

- "Define big profits. Your Inner CEO doesn't know what you mean when you say that."
- "What does *fast* mean? Does it mean three hours, three days, or three weeks?"
- "How much income do you want, and when? Do you want it weekly, monthly, quarterly, yearly? You have to define it."
- "Which relationship, and how, specifically, do you want to improve it? What's the problem?"
- "Your Inner CEO doesn't know what you mean by 'more time with your family.' What do you mean? Do you mean four hours a week? An hour every evening?"
- "What does 'get fantastic results' mean?"

Everything is taken literally, so you do need to be precise about what you ask for. Otherwise, your Inner CEO will look at your request (as anyone else would) and say, metaphorically, "I have no idea what you're talking about," and toss it into the wastebasket.

Clients often ask me, "Why do I need to be so precise with my Inner CEO? She's another part of me, so doesn't she know exactly what I mean at all times?" In some cases she does, but in other cases she doesn't, so a wise strategy is to define *all key words and terms* in your requests to make sure your Inner CEO knows what you mean.

You must be careful, however, not to limit the response options by being too precise. While you should be precise about what you want, *leave the response options open-ended* so you don't limit the ability of your Inner CEO (and others in the invisible network) to help you.

What does "open-ended response options" mean? When your requests for help are approved and invisible network activity is initiated, your Inner CEO will be led through exact-match responses to people, ideas, resources, techniques, and strategies that are possible pathways to your ideal outcome. Your Inner CEO will then choose the best option for you.

Suppose you're crafting a request for help to double the sales of your business. If your Inner CEO approves your request, you'll end up receiving the best help available to do that, no matter what shape it takes. However, because all requests receive exact-match responses, if you narrow the possible delivery options too much (because you think it should manifest in a specific way), you may not produce your ideal outcome because it may not be possible within the artificial limitations you applied.

For example, if your request said "I want to double sales by selling 56 more of item ZX55," "I want to double sales by adding four more outside salespeople," or "I want to double sales in X way," can you see how this might limit you? What if the best way to produce the doubled-sales result was different from the pathway you specified?

You might be thinking to yourself, "Well, if I narrow things too much by asking for the wrong response option, my Inner CEO can just ignore me and deliver the better option." From my experience, that doesn't happen. Always remember, the way the system works, everything is taken literally.

In the same vein, there are times when it would be wise to ask for help to find the perfect candidate for your job opening or to fill the need you have for a vendor or contractor but not wise to ask for help to hire a specific individual or firm.

If you decide, "I need to have this particular guy or girl," "I want to do business with this particular contractor," "I want to do business with this particular vendor," you limit the response options and the results you can produce. The other more powerful option is, "I have this need. I want to produce that result. Help me to find the best way to do that."

The bottom line, again, is this: There is often a huge difference between what you think you want, from the limited perspective of your conscious mind, and what you really want, from the broader perspective of your Inner CEO, who knows about your mission and life purpose and who can tap into the vast resources available through the invisible network.

I'm glad that I don't have to try to make all these kinds of decisions myself. While I have a healthy respect for myself, my intelligence, and my abilities, I'm also crystal clear on how limited my perspective and access to information and resources is.

Always leave the door open to get what you really want. You want to get the result that's best for you and what's genuinely going to have the most positive impact on your situation.

There's another kind of door you want to leave open, too. For example, you ask your Inner CEO to help you earn $250,000 a year and your request is approved. You will receive exact-match responses through the network and be led to the best pathway to earning $250,000 a year.

But let's say it was possible for you to earn $275,000 a year, $300,000 a year, $500,000 a year, or $1 million a year in the same job or with the same amount of time and effort. Because everything in the invisible network is taken literally, when you say, "I want your help to earn $250,000 a year," that's what you're going to get help with if it's approved. Even if $250,000 a year is what you want, you're still limiting yourself by asking for it. The way to leave the door open is to add wording like this to your requests: "or more," "or sooner," "or better."

For example, if you say in your request, "I want to make $250,000 a year *or more*," the simple act of adding the two words "or more" dramatically changes what happens when your request gets into the exact-match world of your Inner CEO and the invisible network.

Sometimes, you have to make your requests open-ended in a slightly different way. At other times, you can say, for example, "Hey, I have an opening for a vice president of sales, and I really think this particular individual would be the best person to fill the job. So if I'm right on that, help me to get him or her. If I'm not, then I'm open to whoever else you feel is better."

In the case of my Blue Ocean Software IPO request, I divided it into the pieces I mentioned, but I also left it open-ended in case we were wrong about one or more of the pieces. It was important to divide it into pieces, however, because if I just said "Help us have a successful IPO," there would have been fewer potential exact matches in the network. But if I ask for help to do a successful IPO with "successful IPO" divided into six specific parts, I can get exact matches on any combination of the parts or on all of them, and I have a better chance of producing my ideal outcome.

So, the bottom line is to be as precise as you can in terms of what you want, but always leave the potential response options completely open-ended.

Guideline 5: Write Your Requests as Stand-Alone Documents

As you write your requests for help, assume that your Inner CEO knows nothing beyond what you actually say in the request. Include all the detail that's needed for her to make a decision about granting your request from what's contained in the request itself.

If you wanted an important business project to be green-lighted or funded by a boss, partner, or banker, would you completely state your case with lots of detail and supporting documentation, or would you be general and vague and expect the CEO to do a lot of work to figure out what you're talking about and asking for? You'd tell a complete and documented story, wouldn't you? It works the same way with sending requests for help to your Inner CEO.

There is only one exception to this guideline, illustrated with an example from my life. I have a particular lifestyle package I've previously defined in a very long and detailed request. I call it my "Writers Life." Because I previously created the definition of that term and documented it in detail to my Inner CEO, I can use the term in other requests without taking the time to define it again.

Unless you've previously defined something that's complex and detailed, be sure to write your requests as if they're stand-alone documents. Assume your Inner CEO is going to pick the document out of her in-box, read it, and make a decision based only on what's there on the paper. Certainly your Inner CEO has access to other information about you, but always tie your camel; and if you provide all the information necessary for your Inner CEO to make a decision, you cover all your bases and leave nothing to chance.

Guideline 6: Be as Optimistic as You Like, but Remain Realistic

Like being precise with what you want but leaving response options open-ended, you have to keep a careful balance between being optimistic (asking for help to achieve big goals and thinking anything is possible) and being unrealistic.

In my work with clients and my Ultimate Lifestyle Academy students who are new to *The 11th Element* system, I frequently see people asking their Inner CEOs for help to produce a result such as generating $20,000 to pay off a debt within *one week*. Or someone asks for help to generate a net worth of $10 million within one year, when they're in debt and earning only $20,000 a year.

I generally reply by saying, "Anything is possible, and I don't want to unnecessarily limit you, but you have to be realistic. It's okay to ask for anything, but realize that what you're asking for may not be possible from a practical standpoint. Inner CEOs may often seem like magicians or miracle workers, but they still need to do lots of work behind the scenes and through the invisible network to help us, and it can take much more time than you imagine to produce the results you're requesting—assuming your request is approved."

The solution to managing this balancing act is simple: Take a realistic look at your request before sending it to your Inner CEO, and consider scaling down what you're asking for if you feel you may be reaching too high or too fast. In the example of the individual who was in debt and only making $20,000 but wanted a net worth of $10 million, I would have suggested scaling the request down by asking first for help to get out of debt, then to increase annual income, then to build a significant net worth over time. You can always scale things back up later after you get the first installment on what you asked for, but if you reach too high or too fast, your request will most likely be ignored.

The other solution to managing this balancing act is to simply ask for what you want, regardless of how realistic it seems, but add open-ended wording afterward; for example, "Or, if that's not possible from a practical standpoint, please help me do it as quickly as possible."

Guideline 7: Explain Why You Want It

The reason you want your ideal outcome may be obvious. It may not be obvious. But I strongly suggest adding a background statement that tells your Inner CEO why you want the help you're requesting. It can greatly enhance the odds that you'll receive tangible benefits from your requests.

Remember, all requests sent to Inner CEOs and into the invisible network are taken literally. Many times I see clients craft requests asking for help to produce specific results, their requests are turned down by their Inner CEOs, and nothing changes in their lives as a result. However, if those same requests include a reason why background statement, their Inner CEOs might respond to the core benefit that is desired and help them produce another result that gives them that core benefit—even if the manifestation looks different from the outcome originally requested.

For example, suppose you're crafting a request for help to increase your income to $100,000 a year or to find a new job, and your reason for wanting those outcomes is to remove the stress and fear you feel about your current situation. If you just ask for help to increase your income or find the new job and those outcomes aren't in alignment with your mission, your request may be rejected. However, if you also give your reason, you still won't get the $100,000 or the new job if it's not in alignment with your mission, but you may get the real benefit you want, which is to relieve the fear and stress.

Guideline 8: As Appropriate, Ask for a Sign

As you'll see in the next chapter, it's often challenging for your Inner CEO to get you the guidance or help you're seeking, so it's important to ask for a very clear and definite sign of what you need to know or do if your request has been granted.

If you're confused about something, you don't know if you're supposed to go right or left at a fork in the road, or you don't know if you're supposed to do this or that in response to movements in your world, use this wording (or something similar) in your requests: "Give me a knock-me-over-the-head-so-I-can't-miss-it sign. . . ."

Again, everything in your requests for help is taken literally, so if you just ask for help, guidance, or an answer of some kind, it could come in a variety of ways. But if you ask for a knock-me-over-the-head-so-I-can't-miss-it sign, you increase the odds that it will be delivered in a way that you're sure to recognize.

When I explain this to clients and students, I'm often asked, "Why do I need to specify a sign like that? Why doesn't my Inner CEO always deliver information in that manner?" If you wondered that, my answer is that it relates to everything being taken literally, and from my experience, if you ask for a can't-miss-it sign, you'll get better results.

What can such a sign look like? It's different for everyone, and I suggest that you resist the temptation to try to boil it down to simple rules or formulas. But to give you an idea of what other people have experienced, I once got an idea that was accompanied by a snap feeling in my head that I would compare to a rubber band being stretched out to full length, being let go, then snapping back with strong force and a loud sound. Some people get strong sensations in their solar plexus or stomach area. Other people simply feel a strong motivation to do or avoid something. Some people get signs through very intense dreams. Others get a thought or idea that just won't go away for multiple days in a row. Still others hear something in their own mind or from someone else and get a feeling of absolute correctness in their gut that urges them to take action. Still others simply get blocked or experience tremendous resistance every time they attempt to go in a specific direction. Signs can take any shape or form, and you don't want to limit the potential of your Inner CEO to communicate with you by narrowing the options too much. You'll see many examples of signs in later chapters of the book.

Guideline 9: Write Your Requests Using Your Computer and Print Them

If possible, craft your requests on your computer using your word processor. Then save them and print them when you're ready to submit them to your Inner CEO for approval. There are three primary reasons for this. First, for most people, the process of writing, even if you don't like to write or don't think you're good at it, tends to help clarify thinking and communication, and clarity is a valuable thing when it comes to crafting requests for help.

Second, if you're like me, you may start crafting a request on a Monday and send it to your Inner CEO for approval on Wednesday. Then on the following Wednesday something will happen, you'll change your mind about what you asked for, and you'll need to revise your request. If you can open the original document, edit it in your word processor, then save and print it again, it's much easier than if you have to write the whole thing again by hand or another method.

Third, having requests stored on your computer makes it easier to review them as appropriate. After you begin sending such written requests to your Inner CEO for approval I suggest reviewing them periodically to make sure that they're all current. Many times I see clients and students submitting requests for help, forgetting about them, letting weeks pass, and not noticing that events and manifestations in their worlds made their original requests obsolete. If you review your requests frequently and revise them as needed, you increase your power.

In addition, when you review your requests like this, you will see that they fall into four categories:

1. Still waiting for manifestation
2. Need to revise
3. Don't want anymore
4. Already fulfilled (or being fulfilled now)

If I'm still waiting for manifestation, I simply continue waiting. I revise the ones that need to be revised and submit the revised copy to my Inner CEO. I withdraw the ones I no longer want and put them in a "Changed my mind" file so I can review them later. I find that to be fun and interesting. Finally, I put the ones that were fulfilled into a "Got it" file. I then go back to review that file often to celebrate my many victories!

Finally, as you'll see once you begin applying *The 11th Element* system, it's interesting, fun, and educational to go back and look at your requests again after time has passed. If you have an easily accessible record, it's very easy for you to look at how your request-drafting skills have improved, what you asked for, what happened in response, and so on.

Guideline 10: Use a Template to Stay Consistent

Using a specific template helps you draft effective requests. It also helps you stay consistent to make sure you cover all your bases each time.

I use and suggest a specific template in the form of a letter to my Inner CEO. All of my requests are structured as if they're personal letters to my Inner CEO. The structure and wording of the template are very precise and deliberate. They've been created from much experience, and they're very powerful. I recommend that you use the template as is.

Following is the template itself with brief notes; then a detailed discussion of each part is provided. My notes are in parentheses.

Dear _____:
(I strongly suggest having a name for your Inner CEO.)

I'm writing to chat with you about _____.
(Fill in the blank with a short statement introducing what you want.)

Please help me yourself and/or guide into my life the people, ideas, resources, techniques, and strategies I can use to:

1.

2.

3.

4.

(Fill in the numbered items with statements of what you think you want—including as many items as needed to craft an effective request; then add additional detail as appropriate, such as your "reason why I want it" statement.)

From the limited perspective of my conscious mind, this is what I think I want, and I ask that you give me this or something even better.

[Signature]

Like a personal letter, you start out with the salutation, "Dear _____." I recommend that you name your Inner CEO so the process of asking for help feels more personal. Your Inner CEO is your ultimate ally or best friend, so it is important to build a personal relationship with her. There are no good names, bad names, or magical names. The results you produce aren't going to be impacted by what you choose to name your Inner CEO, and your Inner CEO doesn't care what you call her. Just choose a name that's fun, that you resonate with, and that you can use to build a personal relationship with your Inner CEO. If you prefer, you can also ask your Inner CEO what name to use when interacting with her by crafting a request for help with this.

Then begin your request by saying, "I'm writing to chat with you about _____," and fill in the blank with a basic overview of your request—what you want help with. You might say "I'm writing to chat with you about increasing my income," or "I'm writing to chat with you about solving a problem I have with the employee profit-sharing program I'm trying to launch in my company." Just include a simple overview summary statement like you might use in any other sort of letter you'd write.

You start the next sentence with, "Please help me yourself . . ." There are times where your Inner CEO can grant your request without needing to seek help through the invisible network. So you start out by allowing for that possibility with this wording. Because everything is taken literally in the invisible network, this is another way of leaving your response options open-ended.

You continue: ". . . and/or guide me to the people, ideas, resources, techniques, and strategies I can use to . . ." Look carefully at that wording and notice how open-ended it is in terms of what kind of help you can get in response to your request. List the specific thing(s) that you want help with. I like doing that in the form of bullets or numbered items. If you have a large, complex request, divide it into pieces in this section and ask for help with each piece individually.

If there is anything else you want your Inner CEO to know about your request or why you want the specific outcome, put it in the next section of the template.

When you're finished asking for the help you need and you've followed the other guidelines you just learned, add this phrase: "From the limited perspective of my conscious mind, this is what I think I want, and I ask that you give me this or something even better." Again, the wording is very deliberate, very precise, and incredibly powerful. First, when you say, ". . . this is what I think I want," you acknowledge how limited your perspective is, which fosters the valuable sense of humility and nonattachment mentioned earlier. When you say, ". . . I ask that you give me this or something even better," you leave the door open for receiving something even better than what you consciously envision at the time. You close your letter by signing it—just as you would a personal letter.

Every request for help I write is written with this exact template. There are no exceptions to that rule, and I encourage you to use it exactly as written.

Guideline 11: Take Your Time!

When you first discover your Inner CEO and the invisible network and begin focusing on what you want to change or create in your world (especially if you have what seems like an urgent need), it can be very tempting to rush in and craft many requests in a hurry.

Resist that temptation! Take your time to do it right—with careful attention to priorities and thought about defining what you want. It's well worth the wait.

You're working with very powerful forces here, so take your time and proceed with something of a fragile, handle-with-care attitude.

Sometimes I take two or three weeks writing a particular request if it's long and complex or if that's what it takes for me to feel that I have it as clear and complete as possible. Sometimes I do it in a few minutes or an hour. The best crafting time depends on the nature and complexity of the request and your level of mastery with crafting requests.

What I generally say to people about a take-your-time strategy is this: "Follow the guidelines and write a rough draft of your request. Let it sit overnight, go back, read it again, then change things or edit it as you see fit. Repeat that process several times over the following few days or for as many days it takes to get it right. When you honestly feel it's as good as you can possibly make it and as clear as you can possibly get it, send it to your Inner CEO for approval," which we discuss in the next chapter.

The more requests you write, the better you'll get at it, the quicker you'll be able to write them, and the better the results you'll produce. Be patient, and you'll get there quickly enough.

Examples of How to Craft a Request

Following are several examples of how to pull the guidelines together to craft requests with maximum potential for results. The examples are taken from my own projects and the projects of clients. Each one led to tremendously positive results. Your focus and desire will probably be to produce outcomes different from the ones you see in these examples, but it doesn't matter. The same principles apply. And if you need to produce similar results, feel free to use these examples as more detailed templates and customize them to your own situation.

Some of the requests are short and simple. Others are longer and more complex. None is perfect. They could all be improved, which is almost always the case with hindsight. These examples suggest possibilities and will help start you down the road toward request-crafting mastery:

Dear _____:

I'm writing today to chat with you about the development of our new branding strategy.

As you know, we're in the process of re-inventing the company, our marketing messages, image, focus, and brand. As a result, I need to define a powerful new brand strategy and implement it in a cost-effective way. By "powerful," I mean that it will support and make possible maintaining our dominance of the low end of our market, while simultaneously moving upstream into the middle tier.

Therefore, please help me yourself and/or guide me to the people, ideas, resources, techniques, and strategies I can use to:

1. *Develop a cohesive brand strategy* we can leverage indefinitely, scaling with the company as it grows. This would include a creative execution (tagline) from which the rest of the company's efforts will be launched.

2. *Internally implement that strategy* with things such as branded community programs, staff programs, product positioning and procedures, and so forth.

3. *Externally implement that strategy* with marketing and sales programs, public relations activities, trade shows, Web issues, advertising, selection of third-party vendors, and so on.

4. *Get approval from our CEO* and buy-in from the rest of the company on the strategy and implementation plan.

(*continued*)

5. *Achieve these goals as quickly as possible,* but preferably within 120 days.

6. *Thoroughly enjoy the process.* I love doing this kind of creative work and want your help to enjoy every minute of it!

From the limited perspective of my conscious mind, this is what I think I want, and I ask that you give me this or something even better.

[Signature]

Dear _____:

I'm writing to chat with you about our third quarter that's coming up. As you know, we have another very aggressive sales goal to hit for the quarter: $11 million (or more), with profits of $5.5 million (or, preferably, more). I need your help to achieve that goal!

I'm open to any kind of help you can provide us to achieve those goals, and as I see it, we need your help directly and/or guidance to the people, ideas, resources, techniques, and strategies we can use to do the following within this time frame:

1. Increase the number of new customers we create through marketing and referrals.
2. Increase the size of the average sale to new customers.
3. Increase our sales of products and services to existing customers.

As I see it, to do 1 to 3 above, we need to do the following, but I'm open to anything you see that will help us meet or beat our goals:

- Effectively execute our direct mail and online marketing models. (Please watch over and help Billy with this.)
- Isolate and open up entirely new marketing revenue streams (such as joint ventures).
- Help our international resellers improve their execution of our marketing model.
- Create and automate the execution of a proactive referral program that generates the maximum possible number of referrals.
- Launch the planned newsletter to customers, structure it in the best way to support the meeting or exceeding of our

(continued)

goals, and fill it with content that provides value to our customers and leads to maximum credibility and sales for us.

- Help the salespeople sell more Enterprise and add-ons to new customers.
- Help the salespeople sell more upgrades, add-ons, support contracts, and support renewals to existing customers.
- Help the salespeople make as many outgoing sales calls as possible to follow up on the tremendous number of leads we generate.
- Help us recruit and bring on board one or more heavy hitter outside salespeople who can help us close more $100,000+ deals. "Heavy hitter" means salespeople who have successful track records selling big-ticket products like ours into the middle-tier niche of our market and who resonate well with our company culture and brand.
- Help us develop the tools and strategies we need to help the heavy hitters close three or more (preferably more) $100,000+ deals every month.
- I want to perform my part of this while maintaining the gentle schedule I have now, retaining a sense of joy and fulfillment of the process and work, and continuing my enjoyment of the people I work with.

To the extent you can, please work with the Inner CEOs of all prospects, employees, new-hire candidates, vendors, and contractors to help us meet or, preferably, exceed our goals. I'm also open to anything else you can do to help us meet or, preferably, exceed our goals.

From the limited perspective of my conscious mind, this is what I think I want, and I ask that you give me this or something even better.

[Signature]

Dear _____:

I'm writing to chat with you about building our network of international resellers. To launch this new program and make it successful, I need to hire an international marketing manager as soon as possible. Because I've never built a program like this before, I need your help!

Please help me yourself and/or guide me to the people, ideas, resources, techniques, and strategies I can use to:

- Attract the perfect candidate into our orbit. When I say "perfect candidate," I mean that I prefer someone who has already successfully built a reseller program similar to the one we have planned, someone I will enjoy working with, who will integrate smoothly into the department, resonate well with the company culture, and who will help us meet or, preferably, exceed our international sales goals—but I'm open to your guidance about the best candidate for us.

- Understand the core skills that are necessary for this person to succeed and be able to effectively probe for verification of those skills in interviews and reference checks—by phone or face to face.

- Recognize the perfect candidate when I find him or her.

- Negotiate a win-win financial and/or relocation package allowing me to actually hire the perfect candidate. By "win-win," I mean that both the company and the new hire feel that they're receiving tremendous value through the transaction.

From the limited perspective of my conscious mind, this is what I think I want, and I ask that you give me this or something even better.

[Signature]

Dear _____:

We need to redesign our web site, which is a big deal for us. Lots of egos and opinions are involved, and because it's the lifeblood of our business, we have to do it right. Please help us get the correct concept for the site. It needs to:

- Satisfy me graphically.
- Satisfy the president graphically.
- Help us consistently increase the number of demo downloads we generate and the sales we close from them.
- Please work with our artist, too, and help him, directly or with my guidance, to get the perfect concept for the design. By "perfect concept," I mean the look, feel, navigation, and flow that are most likely to resonate with our prospects and customers and support us in meeting or exceeding our goals.

This is really important to me, to our president, to our relationship, and to the success of the company. Doing this well will be one of the best gifts I can give the company and my career, so please help!

From the limited perspective of my conscious mind, this is what I think I want, and I ask that you give me this or something even better.

[Signature]

Dear _____ :

I'm writing today to chat with you about my client, _____.

I took them on to help them build their business. They're great people, have a great service, and have targeted a very lucrative niche with tons of potential. As we determined, I need to help them create the following (although I'm open to hearing about anything else that would help me help them achieve their goals):

- A new company name that telegraphs the benefits of the new brand we'll develop.
- A white paper designed to educate, motivate, and sell their services after inviting them to request a free consultation.
- A new sales letter designed to generate requests for the white paper.
- A new web site designed to generate requests and deliver the white paper online.
- A direct mail strategy for generating white paper requests.
- An online marketing strategy for generating Web visitors and white paper requests.

I've done a lot of research, I understand their market, and I feel very confident about this project, but I ask that you help me yourself or guide me to the people, ideas, resources, techniques, and strategies I can use to create the above resources and materials to ensure success of this project. By "success" I mean:

- We create a marketing machine that delivers consistent results, predictable results, and strong profits with a multiplier of three or more (preferably more).

(continued)

- They build their sales and profits so they get the funding and additional management team they need to execute the rest of their business plan.

I like these people. I believe in them and what they do. I want to help them. However, as you know, I have a lot on my plate right now and almost didn't take them on for fear of stretching myself too thin. I need your help to stay as focused and productive as possible, keep the pace of work gentle, draw and maintain my boundaries effectively, and enjoy the work. You know how I define focus, productive, gentle pace, and boundaries from previous requests.

From the limited perspective of my conscious mind, this is what I think I want, and I ask that you give me this or something even better.

[Signature]

Dear _____:

I'm writing to chat with you about helping Blue Ocean Software launch a successful IPO in the spring of next year, market conditions allowing, or at another best time as you see fit. By "successful," I mean an IPO that generates the highest initial stock price (to maximize shareholder value and minimize dilution), attracts a wide array of investors and market makers to support minor ups and downs in stock price over time, and maintains—as much as possible—a strong, growing stock price over time.

We're open to any pathway you suggest to a successful IPO, and as we see it, on top of continuing to produce extraordinary sales and profit results (which were addressed in a separate request), we need to do the following to launch a successful IPO:

- *Align with a top-tier venture capital firm.* We don't need their money, but we do need their help to open the doors to the top-tier investment bankers. Please help us find the one best positioned to help us succeed as defined above.

- *Get two to three heavy hitters to join our board of directors.* By "heavy hitters," I mean directors who have the necessary track record and experience to help us build the company and who also give us the credibility to stand head and shoulders above the other companies wanting to launch IPOs at the same time.

- *Create a strong and positive buzz about the company in the financial press and community.* We have a great story to tell, and we want to get it out there to support the overall effort and have maximum impact, but we need help to find the best way to do this.

(continued)

- *Align with a top-tier investment banker to complete the public offering.* If we're going to do this, we're committed to doing it with the best of everything, including the most successful, skilled, connected, and prestigious investment banker who can help us attract investors and become an invaluable strategic partner in identifying and closing deals for acquisitions and so on.

- *Choose the best timing.* Because the IPO process takes approximately six months from initial green light to IPO (but can be sped up or lengthened once started) and because we want the launch to take place under the most favorable stock market conditions, we need your help (to the extent to which you can provide it) to time the start of the six-month process and the actual launch to best advantage. Please guide us in making these two key decisions.

- *Have a blast!* We're told that going public is a wild ride with many rewards and possible pitfalls. We're not used to being looked at under a microscope by outsiders or feeling pressure from the outside to produce results, all of which is part and parcel of the IPO process. So please help us navigate through this "mine field" and thoroughly enjoy the march and the launch itself. We want this to be a blast and a most memorable event!

From our limited perspectives, this is the kind of help we need, and we ask that you give us this kind of help or other help if you see additional opportunities to help us produce the ideal outcome of a successful IPO as defined above.

[Signature]

Dear _____:

I'm writing to chat with you about my network marketing business. As you know, I became involved with _____ to create another stream of income to supplement my salary ($100,000 a year) with the intent of equaling or exceeding that income from _____, quitting my job, and going into the _____ business full time within 12 months or sooner. I need your help to do this.

I'm open to any way to do this you see as best, and as I see it, to produce this outcome, I need you to please help me yourself and/or guide me to the people, ideas, resources, techniques, and strategies I can use to:

- Find the best tools and most effective strategies (that match my personality and are enjoyable) to help me recruit additional distributors, get them up and running quickly, keep them motivated and on track (especially at the start), and encourage them to faithfully apply "the system" to continue the growth of their business (and mine). I would prefer to do this by getting a top-performing mentor within (preferably in my upline) or even outside the company if that's best, to help me, but I'm open. By "top performing," I mean I'd prefer someone who started under circumstances similar to where I am now, generated a consistent yearly income of $100,000 or more for two years or more, and continues to generate that much or more to this day—but I'm open to what you think is best.

- Help me follow his or her advice and system, keep myself disciplined, motivated, and on track (especially if it takes a

(continued)

while to see significant results), and keep me faithfully applying his or her system until I reach my goal.

- Help me attract the right people to join my team downline, help me achieve my goals, and help themselves achieve theirs, while all having a lot of fun. I will let you define the "right people" as I think you know best.

If there are additional tools and strategies I can use to meet or, preferably, exceed my goals, beyond what I learn from my mentor, please help me to see, find, and use them.

Finally, because I'll be starting out with _____ part time while keeping my 9 to 5 job, there will be the potential of working many hours. I need your help to get as much done as possible with the limited hours I have to invest in this business and to help me stay in balance as much as possible. By "balance," I mean to enjoy the process, still get as much rest as I need to stay healthy and happy, still have a lot of fun in life, and continue spending as much quality time as possible with my friends. I'm willing to invest time here but not at the expense of my overall quality of life. Because you know better than I what the optimal lifestyle is for me, I leave this in your hands to help me as you see fit.

From the limited perspective of my conscious mind, this is what I think I want, and I ask that you give me this or something even better.

[Signature]

Dear _____:

I'm writing to chat with you about my quota. As you know, I need to generate $250,000 in sales for the third quarter, and I'm a bit behind schedule. I have my ideas on what I need to do to catch up and actually exceed my quota in the time I have left, but I'm open to any pathway, and I need your help.

Please help me yourself and/or guide me to the people, ideas, resources, techniques, and strategies that can help me exceed the $250,000 I need.

From the limited perspective of my conscious mind, this is what I think I want, and I ask that you give me this or something even better.

[Signature]

Dear _____:

I'm writing to chat with you about starting an Internet business. I see so many people around me making good money on the Internet, and I want to join the club. But I don't know what kind of business to start or the best way to get it up, running, and making money.

I'd like your help to select and start a business that:

- I'd enjoy running.
- Aligns with my life purpose.
- I can start part time and build from there.
- Has enough potential to consistently earn me $10,000 a month (or more) in net take-home pay per month in 12 months (or fewer).
- Provides a product or service that others find truly valuable.
- Integrates well into my current work schedule, family life, and a healthy lifestyle (I'll let you define "healthy" for me).

I'm sure there's more I should be asking for help with here, but I'll leave the rest up to you because you know what's best for me.

From the limited perspective of my conscious mind, this is what I think I want, and I ask that you give me this or something even better.

[Signature]

The following is the actual request I sent to *my* Inner CEO to generate $209,698 over a 10-month period, easily repay $153,000 in debt, and complete my recovery from my seven-year bout with Murphy's Law. Note that my request-crafting skills have evolved since I wrote this one, but I want you to see it exactly as I wrote it then. It would look different if I were crafting it today.

Dear Inner CEO:

I need to have a chat with you about my financial situation, income-generating options, and career as things have evolved and changed since I last communicated with you.

For ease of writing, I'm going to use "me" and "I" although it should be understood that in most cases, I'm referring to both my wife Cecily and me.

In general, I'm asking for you to help me with the following:

1. Guide me to the people, ideas, resources, opportunities, actions, clients, and/or whatever else it takes to accomplish the following goals while staying in total alignment with who I really am and how I really want to live, having maximum fun, happiness, joy, and minimal stress through the process.

2. Or, if it's not part of my purpose to grant these requests, then please make your reasons clear to me so I can understand and move in another direction with clarity, peace, and confidence.

3. If it is part of my purpose, but there are blockages preventing my progress, please help me to release or change them.

(continued)

4. On top of all these requests, please show me the way to get to the absolute core of the issue and once and for all quiet or eliminate the desire I still seem to have to "spend, spend, spend" (even if I don't have the money), which has gotten me in so much trouble.

Here is what I want: What I really want is my "Writer's Life" as I've described in another letter to you. I believe that I'm moving toward that lifestyle, that it's my destiny to do so after I've evolved and cleared out more layers of programming that no longer serve me.

But I also recognize that it might be a while, so I need to create a new career and/or income-generating scenario that works for me while I'm waiting for my Writer's Life to become a reality. Here are the two areas I need help with:

1. *Debts:* I'd like your help to:
   a. Easily, in as stress-free a manner as possible and as quickly as possible, pay off the remainder of what we owe to Cecily's father, preferably on or before 12/31 of this year.
   b. Easily, in as stress-free a manner as possible and as quickly as possible, pay off the $5,000 loan from my mother, preferably on or before 12/31 of this year, too.
   c. Easily, in as stress-free a manner as possible and as quickly as possible, pay off the $80,000 Northern Trust bank note in full, preferably on or before 12/31 of this year.
   d. Easily, in as stress-free a manner as possible and as quickly as possible, pay off, once and for all, never to

(continued)

be reincurred, my credit card debt—preferably on or before 12/31 of this year.

2. *Income generation:* Help me create a situation where I:

   a. Look forward to the work I do every day.

   b. Am primarily responsible for managing projects, tasks, ideas, accounts, or business relationships, but not people.

   c. Generate consistent, there-like-clockwork, take-home pay from whatever source or combined sources, of an absolute minimum of $6,500 a month and, preferably, $10,000 or more a month in income.

   d. Have minimal stress, maximum fun and excitement, feel challenged, do primarily creative work I enjoy and am good at (i.e., writing, marketing, strategizing, communicating, speaking, teaching), at the level I belong (i.e., big picture stuff) while allowing me to stretch myself and grow in my skills, talents, and abilities.

   e. Work in positive environments with/for people who have a can-do attitude, people I like, respect, that I'm compatible with, enjoy working with, who are responsive to my requests and ideas, and so on.

   f. Create a lifestyle where I can work flexible hours and sometimes from home.

On this date, this is what I think I want from the limited perspective of my conscious mind, and I ask that you give me this or something even better.

So be it. Make it so. Amen.

[Signature]

As you can see, the art of crafting requests isn't difficult. Becoming masterful simply requires some common sense, careful following of the guidelines, a slight shift of focus and intent, attention to detail, and practice over time.

You now know how to craft a request for help to produce your ideal outcome. The next step is to send your completed request to your Inner CEO for review—with the ultimate goal of getting it approved and sent into the network so you can receive the help you want. In Chapter 5, you will discover a simple and fun system for doing that.

5

Turbocharging Your Engines

People of talent resemble a musical instrument more closely than they do a musician. Without outside help, they produce not a single sound, but given even the slightest touch, and a magnificent tune emanates from them.[1]

— Franz Grillparzer, 1791–1872

This chapter discusses the third, fourth, fifth, and sixth steps in the process of applying *The 11th Element* system:

Step 3: Submit your request to your Inner CEO for approval.

Step 4: Receive approval.

Step 5: Tap into the invisible network for help.

Step 6: Perform due diligence and make decisions and plans.

Step 3: Submit Your Request to Your Inner CEO for Approval

When you add a turbocharger to certain automobile engines, you get more power from the same amount of gasoline. To add a turbocharger to the engine that drives your business and wealth-building efforts, you must enlist the help and support of your Inner CEO and tap into the tremendous pool of resources available through the invisible network.

Once your request for help has been written, you must submit it to your Inner CEO for approval before invisible network activity can be initiated. To understand the submission process, it is helpful to imagine that your Inner CEO works in a gigantic control room filled with computers, video screens, telephones, intercom systems, cell phones, fax machines, a sound system, and other equipment. You can also imagine that your Inner CEO has a full team of assistants and helpers working with him in the control room to manage projects through to completion.

An excellent visual image of a control room such as this appears in the movie *The Truman Show,* and it would be valuable for you to watch that movie as soon as possible to support your integration of this material. It should be available in any movie rental or sales outlet. As you'll see in later chapters, *The Truman Show* provides other excellent visual images that will help you to apply *The 11th Element* system. You might even want to buy your own copy and watch it multiple times.

From within the control room, your Inner CEO monitors everything you think, everything you say, everything that is said to you, everything you feel, and everything that happens in your environment on a daily basis. From the control room, research is done using the invisible network search engines and other available resources, requests for help are sent into the invisible network, responses are processed, negotiations are conducted, agreements are made, plans are written, and projects are managed to completion.

The control room is operational 24 hours a day, 7 days a week. It's a very busy place!

Your Inner CEO is always looking for ways to help you, but a tremendous amount of information flows into the control room about you, your life, and the ongoing management of projects. There's a lot of noise, and it's often difficult for your Inner CEO to know when you're asking for help and what kind of help you really want.

If you could put a tape recorder inside your head for one day, record everything you experienced, then play it back and listen to all the things you said to yourself, all the things you thought, all the things you said to other people, and so on, you'd be hopelessly confused about what was going on in your life. We change our minds all the time. Something happens, we have an instant emotional reaction and say or think something, then calm down and say or think something else 20 minutes later. We say one thing to one person on a specific subject, then say something entirely different about that same subject to another person on another day.

For example, you might have a bad day and think or say to yourself, "I hate this job. Get me out of here," "I hate my boss. I wish he'd get fired," or "I wish I were single again." Would you want your Inner CEO to take such thoughts or words seriously and take action about them? No. But consider how much dialog like this goes on in your life and what a challenge it would be for your Inner CEO to understand your true wants, needs, and intentions.

You might think, "Well, my Inner CEO knows I'm just mad and I don't mean those things," and sometimes that's true, but other times, it isn't. At other times, it's genuinely difficult to sort out what you mean, what you don't mean, or what's a passing fancy or the result of a mood. You want to eliminate all possibility for error or misunderstanding and make your communication with your Inner CEO as clear and direct as possible.

The noise level in the control room is also the explanation for why the traditional 10-element techniques work sometimes but not other times. When they do work for someone who's not using *The 11th Element* system, it's because their request for help somehow got through the noise to their Inner CEO, the Inner CEO approved it, and he took action. But the request got through the noise randomly and accidentally—not in a systematic way. You want a simple, quick, and systematic way of getting through the noise and being able to say to your Inner CEO whenever you want, "Hey, I need help with this. I need help now!"

Two request-sending techniques apply to different scenarios in your daily life. In the first scenario, your request isn't urgent, there's no immediate need, and you have time to write a request using the 11 guidelines presented in Chapter 4. In the second scenario, something is happening in the heat of the moment, you have an immediate need for help, and you don't have time to follow the guidelines and write a request.

Before I explain the techniques, keep in mind that your ultimate goal in both scenarios is to create a code system between you and your Inner CEO so that he instantly knows you just sent a request for help, and he needs to drop everything and consider it on the spot.

When I was growing up, I watched many spy and thriller TV shows and movies. In many of them, high-ranking officials had a special red phone in their offices. The red phone was used only for calls from the President of the United States. If the President called, the red phone would light up and make loud beeping sounds to get your immediate attention. To communicate with the President, the officials had one job and one job only—watch the red phone and pick it up immediately if it rang.

That's the kind of arrangement you want with your Inner CEO. You want to have something like that red phone so your Inner CEO, like the government officials in the spy shows, has only one job, too—to watch for a specific signal and instantly respond when calls come in from you.

What I do and what I teach my clients and students to do is to have a *request box*. Mine is a large cookie jar made in the shape of a wizard's head. It doesn't matter what your box is. It can be any-thing you want. It can be something you make or something you buy. I love wizards and collect them, so I chose the cookie jar for my request box. There is no "good" box or "bad" box, and using one versus another won't impact the results you create. You just want your box to be something you enjoy working with, as attrac-tive as you want, and large enough to hold all your requests be-cause the volume will grow over time. Your box should also have enough privacy or security to prevent other people from being able to see what's inside to the degree that's important to you.

When you use a request box, you're saying to your Inner CEO, "Monitor the activity in that box, please. If I put something inside, it means I have a request. It means I need help." Then all your Inner CEO and its staff have to do is watch your request box. They don't have to sort through all the noise in your head and your envi-ronment any more. If you put something in your request box, it's the equivalent of the red phone lighting up and buzzing with a call from the President of the United States.

After following the 11 guidelines to craft your request for help, print a copy and put it into your request box, which sends it into the control room for your Inner CEO to review. It's really that simple, but you'll be amazed by how powerful the technique is and what happens in response. In one simple and elegant move, you've eliminated one of the biggest obstacles to clear and effec-tive communication with your Inner CEO—getting through all the noise—and you've jumped light years ahead of the effective-ness and efficiency of the 10 traditional elements discussed in Chapter 3.

Once you choose your request box and find a suitable location for it in your home or office, write a simple letter to your Inner CEO telling him, "From now on, when I want to send you mes-sages, and I have requests for help, I'm going to use this box," and describe the box and location. That will serve as an initial signal saying, "Here's our new code. Here's how I'm going to communi-cate with you from now on."

In the second scenario, you're in the heat of the moment and need immediate help, you don't have your request box handy, or you don't have time to craft a request using the 11 guidelines. Even though that situation is different, the same basic concept applies. You need to have some sort of code that helps you get through the noise so you can get your request for help right to your Inner CEO.

Choose a simple signal, a simple but unique physical action, and then tell your Inner CEO, "Whenever I do X, it means I need your attention. It means I need help now." Again, you've given your Inner CEO a simple job—look for the signal!

The signal can be anything, as long as it's consistent and not something you'd normally do in your daily life, which would make it confusing for your Inner CEO. My signal is to take my right index finger, tap the point between my eyebrows three times, and say "Listen now." There's no magic to the tap or those specific words, but the combined result is consistent and unique, so it's a very effective signal and I've been using it for years with fantastic results.

When would you use a signal like that? When you're on a sales call and having trouble overcoming an objection, before or during an important meeting or interview, when asked a question you don't know the answer to (but need to), in an airport to make sure your luggage gets to your destination undamaged, for protection when driving on an icy road, and so on. The options are endless. You'll know when the right time to ask comes. You'll just need to remember to actually use the signal and ask for the help.

Decide what your signal will be. Give it serious consideration and make sure it's unique. Then write a simple letter to your Inner CEO explaining your choice and plan; for example, "From now on, when I need your help in the heat of the moment and I don't have the time or ability to use my request box, I'm going to do X as a signal to get your attention." Then put the letter into your request box and send it to your Inner CEO.

Does this sound too simple to actually be effective? If that thought crossed your mind, give it a try and you'll see how powerful it is and how much easier it makes things.

Step 4: Receive Approval

Once received, your Inner CEO reviews your requests for help and decides if they will be approved, rejected, or put on hold for future consideration. The decision will be made based on your Inner CEO's careful review of:

- Your big picture life purpose and mission
- Current projects being worked on, and the likely impact that the granting of your request will have on them
- Projects in the queue to be green-lighted in the near future, and the likely impact that the granting of your request will have on them
- Other pertinent details

This process is very similar to what would happen if you were an employee of a company and went into the CEO's office and said, "I'd like money to do X," or "I'd like the time of three people for three months to do Y." In that situation, the CEO would look at the big picture goals of the business, what's going on right now, what the impact would be if he or she invested the money in your project versus another one, what the impact would be if the time of the three people was diverted to your project for three months, versus letting them do something else.

Just as in the corporate arena, every request you submit will get a "yes," a "no," or a "maybe later." Sometimes the decisions will be made quickly; at other times, more slowly, just as in the corporate arena. But every request will be reviewed, and a decision will be made on each one as quickly as possible. Remember that your Inner CEO and its staff are very busy in their control room working on hundreds, if not thousands, of projects, and it can take time to complete the analysis required to make a solid decision.

If the decision is "yes," you move on to Step 5. If the decision is "maybe later," your request goes on hold for future consideration and might manifest later. If the decision is "no," it's the equivalent of your request being crumpled up and put in a trashcan. However, the important thing to understand is that when requests get turned down, even though you may be frustrated, disappointed, even angry, they get turned down for very good reasons. A "no" is actually good news, not bad news, because when requests are turned down, it's because those outcomes aren't what you really want. It wouldn't really be in your best interest for those outcomes to manifest, even if you think it would be. In fact, granting such requests would actually introduce negatives into your life that you wouldn't want to experience. Always remember that and keep it in the proper perspective.

Although it doesn't always work that way in the corporate arena, you can be assured of a complete and fair hearing for each of your requests, that a solid and excellent decision will be made, and that there won't be any mistakes. Your Inner CEO is always looking for ways to help you and to grant your requests, but he is charged with an important responsibility—helping you fulfill your life purpose and complete your mission—and that project takes absolute priority over making you happy in the short term.

Step 5: Tap into the Invisible Network for Help

If your request for help is approved, your actual request or a slightly modified version will first be sent into the invisible network. When that happens, other Inner CEOs will reply, much like you might reply to an advertisement in a newspaper or magazine.

Whenever requests for help are sent into the invisible network, if there are people who can help you, they will respond. It's an automatic process, different from the conscious level where you might need help, put the word out, and others who could help you might or might not see it; and if they do see it, they might or might not respond. If a request goes into the invisible network and there's somebody out there who can help you, their Inner CEO will see your request, respond, initiate a dialogue, and if they're chosen by your Inner CEO from all the available options, they will provide the help you requested.

Your Inner CEO or its staff will also do research using the invisible network search engines and tap into other invisible network resources looking for the best people and solution(s) for you. They will review the requests and messages other people have sent into the network to see if anybody has already posted something that might be helpful to you. Like the corporate arena, they will open their metaphorical Rolodexes and contact their friends, associates, other Inner CEOs, and control room staff members they've worked with before. Every possibility and option will be considered.

The goal is to make contacts, find potential candidates for the various tasks that create your outcome, and gather all the information needed to isolate the possible pathways you could navigate to jump your gap and produce your ideal outcome in the most effective and efficient way.

Step 6: Perform Due Diligence and Make Decisions and Plans

Once information has been gathered by tapping into the invisible network, all the options and possibilities that were gathered in the previous step will be reviewed carefully as your Inner CEO looks for the best people and solution(s) for you.

If there are multiple people, ideas, resources, techniques, and strategies that could help you, the best one(s) will be chosen. If people are being considered to play specific roles in the manifestation of your outcome, their metaphorical work history and references are checked and verified. They might be interviewed. This process is very similar to the process of hiring an employee or contractor in the corporate arena, except it's much faster; your Inner CEO and his staff have access to the unblemished truth about everyone and everything, which makes decision making infinitely easier.

In addition, your Inner CEO might run different simulations. For example, there are two people who could theoretically do a great job of helping you produce a specific outcome. Your Inner CEO might run several "what would happen if" simulations to do his best to predict which one might provide the most help for you. You can expect your Inner CEO and his staff to be more thorough and complete in their analysis than anything you might be able to imagine from your own perspective. It's really amazing what goes on inside the control rooms!

Once the best options and people are chosen, the best timing for manifestation must be selected, and all the various aspects of the manifestation plan (including people's schedules) must be co-ordinated. Selecting the best timing for manifestation is another major challenge, and it's something that needs to be revised on an ongoing basis as things change in the world. For example, throughout history, wars have had both positive and negative im-pact on personal and economic issues. If the timing to manifest a specific result was chosen before a war broke out, the timing might have to be reconsidered based on the events the war set into motion.

In another vein, if William Johnson's Inner CEO agreed to pro-vide a specific service to you on a specific date to help you produce your ideal outcome and something changes in Johnson's life, caus-ing him to speed up or delay his contribution, your Inner CEO might have to adjust your time line as well. This type of scenario plays itself out frequently in our personal lives and the corporate arena and should be familiar to you.

Once the best timing is chosen, agreements will be made and action plans will be created—just as would happen in the corporate arena when a project is being managed.

Sometimes the due diligence, decision making, and planning process is short, and your outcome manifests quickly. Other times, it's a very long and drawn-out process. That's why you must have pa-tience when you apply *The 11th Element* system. Although easier said than done, it's a critical part of applying the system.

Many people, when they first discover *The 11th Element*, begin their journey with the idea that Inner CEOs have unlimited power and can just snap their fingers to manifest results effortlessly. It doesn't work that way. If the request is simple and within the power of your Inner CEO to grant without needing outside help, it can look magical, effortless, and instant, but many of your requests will be far more complicated than they may appear to you, and they will take work and time to analyze, consider, plan for, and manifest. The important thing is managing your expectations, especially when you're starting out with *The 11th Element* system.

The next and final step in the system is for your ideal outcome to actually manifest, which is the subject of the next chapter.

Making the Jump to Warp Speed

For wisdom requires the discerning, the listening to, the acknowledgment of nudges and notions, of senses and sensations, of the minute and what we often mistakenly assume is the mundane. Wisdom means listening to the still, small voice, the whisper that can be easily lost in the whirlwind of busyness, expectations, and conventions of the world.[1]

—Jean Blomquist

The intuitive mind is a sacred gift and the rational mind is a faithful servant. We have created a society that honors the servant and has forgotten the gift.[2]

—Albert Einstein

This chapter describes the final step in the process of applying *The 11th Element* system:

Step 7: Manifest the outcome.

I'm a big fan of science fiction shows and movies such as *Star Trek* and *Star Wars*. Usually, in these kinds of shows, spaceships have two speeds. One is the cruising speed used to travel under normal conditions. Warp speed or light speed is used when the ship has to travel long distances very quickly.

Sometimes spaceships go to warp speed, and the crew reaches their destination in two seconds. At other times—even at warp speed—it takes days, weeks, or even much longer to get somewhere if the distances are large enough. In our discussion of *The 11th Element, warp speed* means you're going to get there faster than you would at cruising speed, but it doesn't necessarily mean that you're going to get there instantly or what you might define as "fast." The actual speed, as we've discussed, is based on what's revealed through the due diligence, decision making, and planning process.

After you become clear on your ideal outcome, you've crafted your request for help, your Inner CEO has granted approval, invisible network activity has been initiated, responses have been processed, decisions have been made, action plans have been created, and the outcome is set to manifest, *then* you're ready to make the jump to warp speed. This means all the resources are in place for you to jump the current gap from where you are now to where you really want to be. But before you can actually make that jump, one additional challenge must be overcome.

For example, assume that the action plan for manifesting your ideal outcome includes your getting three ideas, connecting with two people, and using a specific strategy. Your Inner CEO is in the control room, and she knows what those three ideas are, who the two people are and what they've agreed to do for you, and what the strategy is that you need to execute. So the challenge becomes: How does your Inner CEO let you know the details of the plan? How does she transmit the ideas to you? How does she ensure that you connect with the two people? How does she ensure that you discover the strategy and know how and when to execute it? Again, your Inner CEO doesn't just snap her fingers to execute the plan instantly and completely. As with our daily efforts, the plan must unfold step by step in a linear fashion.

Sometimes getting plan details and to-do items to you is very easy; sometimes it's tough. There are times when your Inner CEO must try multiple times using different approaches before the message gets through. Or, even if you get the message, sometimes unforeseen changes force the plan to be rewritten. If, for example, your Inner CEO set up a meeting between you and Sally Johnson at a party on Saturday night at 6:30, but Sally gets in a car accident and misses the party, your Inner CEO has to go to Plan B and come up with another way to connect with Sally (or someone else to replace her). These kinds of things happen. We live in a complicated, fast-paced world with a lot going on. The best-laid plans don't always manifest in the way that they were meant to.

Sometimes your Inner CEO tries to send you a message about how to execute a specific part of a plan, and you don't receive it. Maybe she gave you a strong feeling in your gut, planted an idea in your brain, but you didn't recognize it as a message. Maybe your Inner CEO tried to send a message through a dream, but you didn't remember it in the morning. Or your Inner CEO sent someone into your life who delivered a message through a conversation with you, but you didn't recognize the message or act on the information. Your Inner CEO must keep trying different approaches to get you the message, and this can get very complex and time consuming. This is another reason why patience is so important.

The request box and the simple signal discussed in Chapter 5 facilitate the flow of information from you to your Inner CEO and help cut through the noise. To improve the flow of information from your Inner CEO to you, however, another strategy is required. You must create *reverse code systems* and leave as many communication channels open as possible.

As obvious as it may sound to you, the key here is to be alert and open-minded and understand that the manifestation of your action-plan steps can come from anyone, anywhere, at any time, possibly in unusual ways you wouldn't expect.

Many people try to run their businesses and build wealth by using logic and intellect alone, which is a very flawed and limited strategy. It's similar to dropping a proposal on the desk of your corporate CEO and saying, "I'd like your approval for X," then going back to your office, closing your door, locking it from the inside, unplugging your phone, turning off your computer, and saying, "Well, where's the response to my proposal?" When you shut off all the communication channels, how is your CEO supposed to reach you?

Your Inner CEO is always trying to get through to send you the approved help you requested. But you need to help her by opening, tuning into, and monitoring as many communication channels as possible—and being very alert to movements in your life.

Now I have some good news and bad news. The good news is that there are strategies you can use to facilitate this process. The bad news is that, unlike the other steps in *The 11th Element* system, I can steer you in the right direction, but I can't give you specific rules or formulas that are guaranteed to work for you when it comes to receiving information and guidance from your Inner CEO as part of manifesting your outcomes. Why? Because you and I (and everyone else reading this book) are very different. We have different personalities, preferences, histories, thought processes, emotional hot buttons, and things we track and notice. A code or signal that gets my attention might not get yours, and vice versa. So you'll need to work with your Inner CEO over time to agree on the codes and communications systems that work for you. And you must be willing to consistently update and revise them over time as needed.

Strategies to Help You Receive Guidance from Your Inner CEO

To improve your ability to receive messages from your Inner CEO, four options are available to consider. Then a variety of examples illustrate how information and guidance flowed from Inner CEOs to other successful and wealthy entrepreneurs so you can see how working with those four options can look and feel. The four options are:

1. Ask for a *general* knock-me-over-the-head sign.
2. Ask for a specific signal.
3. Ask for help to awaken and develop your intuition or sixth sense.
4. Use intuitive counselors until you awaken your own abilities.

Ask for a General Knock-Me-over-the-Head Sign

Recall that in the section on how to craft requests for help (Chapter 4, Guideline 8), we described ways to ask your Inner CEO for a knock-me-over-the-head-so-I-can't-miss-it sign when it was sending you information or guidance. You will find it extremely valuable to incorporate that wording into all your requests.

Ask for a Specific Signal

This is an option you should use with caution, and always leave the response options open-ended; but a very effective strategy can be to ask your Inner CEO to send you a specific signal in response to your requests for help. For example, a friend of mine has a rule that if she tries to go in a particular direction—and that direction might be trying to call somebody on the phone, go somewhere, or buy something—and she gets resistance three times, she interprets that as a no and she stops going in that direction. She calls it her "three-and-out rule." The good thing about that is if you communicate a code like that to your Inner CEO and say, "Look, I'm going to have this three-and-out rule," your Inner CEO can say, "Okay, I'm going to make sure I block you three times if that's the information I want to send you."

The risk with this strategy is that sometimes we experience resistance in life, and there could be repeated resistance to her moving in a direction that isn't an actual message from her Inner CEO. That's why you need to leave the response options open-ended. For example, when using such a code system, you could say, "I'm going to have the three-and-out rule, but if there's ever a time when I get resistance three times and you still want me to keep going, give me a knock-me-over-the-head sign to continue."

One of my clients once asked whether he should go in a particular career direction and specified that if the answer was yes, he would see a yellow rose three times in the following 24 hours. He felt that was a good code because he rarely saw yellow roses. He got that signal and acted accordingly.

Depending on what the specified code is, it might not be possible for your Inner CEO to do what you ask, so, again, you always want to leave the response options open-ended. In this case, you might say "Let me see a yellow rose three times in the next 24 hours, or if that's not possible, then give me another knock-me-over-the-head sign."

You could also say, "If you're going to give me a signal in the form of a thought or feeling or intuition, give me the information and simultaneously give me a little tickle in my throat or stomach." Get creative with this idea and you'll find lots of possibilities that could work for you. If you use this strategy, you have to request signals that are unusual but not so obscure that it would be too difficult for your Inner CEO to do what you ask.

Ask for Help to Awaken and Develop Your Intuition or Sixth Sense

What is intuition? What is the sixth sense or psychic ability? What is gut instinct? What is a sense about something? From the perspective of *The 11th Element,* there's nothing magical or mystical about such concepts. They're simply labels used to describe the process of receiving information and messages from your Inner CEO or through the invisible network. As discussed in Chapter 1, you've received messages from your Inner CEO and through the network many times. You know that it's a real and true source of information, despite the hype and deception that surrounds things such as psychic hot lines and other people pretending to have such abilities.

To communicate with other people in our daily lives, we use telephones, cellular phones, television, radio, modems, fax machines, satellite communications, and so on. All of these systems are based on numbers and frequencies. If you want to reach someone by phone, cell phone, fax, or modem, you have to know the number to dial. To pick up a television station, radio station, or satellite channel, you have to tune a receiver to a particular frequency. All the information and messages flowing through the invisible network use numbers and frequencies, too. You can learn to tune your own receiver to those frequencies and receive information and messages from your Inner CEO and through the network. Like any other skill, it takes time, practice, or a good teacher or mentor. To me, intuition is the ultimate power because it gives you access to the information and resources available through the invisible network, and you now know how powerful those can be. Intuition is a skill that should be considered absolute top priority to develop.

Ken Blanchard, coauthor of *The One Minute Manager* and other best-selling management titles, said, "There is no doubt in my mind that the effective use of intuition in management can help improve the quality of decision-making in organizations."[3]

Frances E. Vaughan, psychologist and author of *Awakening Intuition*, states, "At any given moment, one is conscious of only a small portion of what one knows. Intuition allows one to draw on that vast storehouse of unconscious knowledge that includes not only everything that one has experienced or learned, either consciously or subliminally, but also the infinite reservoir of the collective or universal unconscious, in which individual separateness and ego boundaries are transcended."[4]

Information and messages that come through intuition (*intuitive hits*, as I call them) can come in many forms. At the physical level, intuitive hits come in the form of bodily sensations such as a tickle in the throat, pressure in the solar plexus area, or a snapping sensation in the head. At the emotional level, they come in the form of feelings or *feeling tones*. From my experience, when an intuitive hit is coming from your Inner CEO or through the network, it feels different. It feels somehow cleaner, or more powerful, or clearer. At the mental level, intuitive hits can come to you as pictures, ideas, or voices in your mind. You'll see many specific examples of how intuitive hits contributed to creating breakthroughs, business success, and wealth in the stories that follow later in this chapter.

In his book *The Logic of Intuitive Decision Making*, Weston Agor summarized the results of a four-year study he did with 3,000 business executives in a variety of private and public-sector organizations and management settings. He wrote in the preface to the book: "One of the key findings I report is that top executives in every organization studied are significantly different (statistically) from their subordinates in one key characteristic—*their ability to use intuition to make management decisions.*"[5]

Agor continued, "One significant factor is that top managers often find that traditional analytical techniques (such as Management By Objectives [MBO] or Program Evaluation Review Technique [PERT] forecasting) are not always as useful as they once were for guiding decisions. This is so because top executives now have to make major decisions in a climate characterized by rapid change and at times also laden with crisis events. Frequently, totally new trends are emerging which make linear projection models based on past trends either inaccurate or misleading."[6]

Agor also wrote, "Carl Jung, the famous psychologist, found in his research that managers who become skilled in the use of their intuition tend to possess particular decision-making skills not normally possessed by others. They:

- See possibilities in any given situation.

- Have a sense or vision of what is coming in the future and how to move their organization in response to it.

- Are adept at generating new ideas and in providing ingenious new solutions to old problems.

- Deal effectively with rapid change and highly complex decision-making situations."[7]

Agor's research showed that intuitive hits are particularly valuable in scenarios where:

- There is a high level of uncertainty
- There is little previous precedent
- Variables are often not statistically predictable
- Facts are limited
- Facts do not clearly point the way to go
- Time is limited, and there is pressure to be right
- There are several plausible alternative solutions to choose from, with good arguments for each

Do those scenarios sound familiar to you? Aren't those the very scenarios you must deal with on a daily basis as you work to build business success and wealth?

Agor continued, "At the same time, these executives state that when they make mistakes, it is primarily due to the fact that they fail to use their intuition effectively to guide their decisions. They allow themselves to get 'off course' by letting other factors such as their own ego involvement get in the way of the normal flow of their intuitive radar."[8]

Michael Dell wrote, "You also need to embrace an experimental attitude in making decisions. Sometimes you can't wait for all the data to present themselves before making a decision. You have to make the best decision you possibly can based on your experience, intuition, available data, and assessment of risk."[9]

During the nearly five years we worked together, I saw Russ Hobbs, CEO of Blue Ocean Software, make hundreds of decisions based on intuition or what he called his "gut instinct." Many of those decisions went against the grain of conventional wisdom, the advice of the experts, or the strongly voiced opinions of his management team.

Every time the information truly came from his intuition, the decision ended up being right on. I say "truly came," because many people (including Russ) believe that information or feelings they're receiving are coming from intuition when the actual source is something else (fear, deep seeded beliefs, or *fast logic*). This kind of misinterpretation, when combined with action, *can* lead to mistakes that cause extra work for your Inner CEO, who must make course corrections. Your Inner CEO can always steer you back on course, but it's wise to minimize the number of course corrections because the time and energy required to make them can be better spent on other projects.

You must work with your Inner CEO to develop your *sorting skill*, so you can differentiate intuitive hits from other forms of information. It takes the crafting of requests for help, time, and effort, but the skill can be developed and enhanced if you're serious and committed.

Learning to awaken and develop your intuition is beyond the scope of this book, but to begin the process, simply follow the guidelines and craft a request for help to awaken and develop your intuitive skills. For additional resources to help you do it, visit this page on my web site: http://www.11thelement.com/intuition.html.

Use Intuitive Counselors until You Awaken Your Own Abilities

As you work to develop your own intuitive skills, it can be extremely valuable to seek out the services of intuitive counselors. There are people out there who were either born with their intuitive skills developed to a high level or who spent many years proactively working to develop the skill. I have used intuitive counselors at many times in my career, and I continue to use them now when I need additional guidance, when I'm having trouble sorting out all the information I'm receiving, or to get confirmation of my own intuitive hits. There are several counselors I work with regularly, and I'm always discovering new ones through my daily efforts. For the latest list of the intuitive counselors I can endorse because of my personal experience with them, see this page on my web site: http://www.11thelement.com/intuitives.html.

Learning to Process Messages from Your Inner CEO

The process of receiving information and guidance from Inner CEOs is an ongoing challenge for the reasons discussed earlier. It's not something you can boil down to a few simple rules, formulas, or signals, then get lazy, forget about it, and think you have it handled for the rest of your life.

There's always a certain amount of mystery to the process, and it always takes creativity, effort, and being alert and open to intuitive hits and movements in your life. You can reduce the mystery, however, and increase the odds of recognizing and receiving messages by using these four options and working with your Inner CEO to create the strategies that work best for you.

You can compare the process of receiving help from your Inner CEO to dancing with a partner when you're learning the steps for the first time. When dancing, the person leading makes a move, then the partner makes a move in response. Then the person leading makes a move, and the partner makes another move, and so on. At first the partners are awkward, but over time and with practice, they get in sync and their movements become smooth and graceful. It just takes desire, work, and practice.

You can see a variety of examples of how the dance between you and your Inner CEO works by watching *The Truman Show* movie. The comparison of the relationship between Truman and the director of the TV show in the movie isn't a perfect match for the relationship between you and your Inner CEO (there are deceptive, limiting, and manipulative influences at work in the movie that aren't mirrored in your relationship with your Inner CEO), but the scenes will stimulate some valuable thought processes in your brain and help you apply *The 11th Element* system.

If you use the communication options I suggested, if you get an insight, or if something happens in your life—and you're not sure if it was a message from your Inner CEO—you can always use the request-crafting template and write a request for help, for example,

"I asked you for help on X. I asked you for a sign, and Y happened. I'm not sure if that's a sign from you or not. If it is, give me another knock-me-over-the-head sign as confirmation."

Examples of How Information and Guidance Can Be Manifested

Now that you have some general communication options and guidelines for receiving information from your Inner CEO, specific examples from my life and the lives of very successful and wealthy entrepreneurs will show you how requests for help manifested and how information flowed from our Inner CEOs.

The first example comes via Richard Branson, one of the most successful entrepreneurs in the United Kingdom. He's a billionaire, is very famous, and has a lot of flair and style. I'm a big fan of his. Two of Branson's biggest successes that contributed to his building great wealth are Virgin Records and Virgin Airways.

Virgin Records was actually created as an accident. At one point in Branson's early career, he was trying to launch a magazine, and the magazine was failing. The company had severe cash flow problems. One evening, he was at his home with his employees, brainstorming about what they could do to get some immediate cash to save the business.

In that brainstorming session, Branson suddenly had the idea to sell discount records by mail order. He'd never thought about selling discount records; the concept had crossed his mind for the first time at that moment. It wasn't anything he'd previously been interested in, but suddenly it became clear to him that people were buying more and more records, they were available only at full retail price in retail stores, and selling them at a discount by mail could be a successful strategy.

The idea "popped into his head" completely out of nowhere, they undertook the project, it became a successful strategy, and one thing led to another. That one idea led Branson to start his own record label: Virgin Records. Where did that idea come from? It was a message from his Inner CEO designed to steer him in the direction of a major project that was part of his mission—a project that his Inner CEO was working on independently—outside Branson's conscious awareness.

A similar chain of events led to the formation of Virgin Airways. Branson was very busy running Virgin Records and other businesses he'd started. Again, he had no conscious interest in running an airline and had never even thought about running an airline before. But one afternoon, Randolph Fields called him to inquire if he'd be interested in buying an airline. At first, Branson ignored the call. But Fields persevered, and finally Branson agreed to review a written proposal.

Writing in *Richard Branson, The Authorized Biography*, Mick Brown said this about the airline proposal from Fields: "As Branson would have been the first to acknowledge, common sense dictated that he avoid it at all costs. He knew nothing about airlines, and even less about Randolph Fields. It was nothing to do with the record industry, or entertainment of any sort, and thus a radical departure from the Virgin principle of expanding into related fields. Furthermore, the investments necessary to make an airline work could, theoretically, drag Virgin into bankruptcy."[10]

Yet, a mere 48 hours later, Branson signed an agreement to go into the airline business. Why? Why did he go against logic and common sense and take such a huge risk? Because he received a clear signal from his Inner CEO to do it, and once again, his Inner CEO had been working on a major project without Branson's awareness. Why? Because the project was part of his mission and life purpose!

Throughout his career on the road to his billion-dollar success story, you see examples like this with Branson—examples of people, ideas, resources, techniques, and strategies popping out of nowhere to help him, examples of Branson having feelings or making decisions that defied logic and common sense, bringing him tremendous successes.

Or consider Nike, the sports shoe company. Nike was originally a partnership between two men, Bill Bowerman and Phil Knight. Bowerman, the track coach at the University of Oregon, had a passion for creating his own unique and often revolutionary track shoes to help his athletes improve their performance.

One of the biggest breakthroughs Nike had in its early years—a breakthrough that led to a huge, successful line of shoes for them—came in an unusual way. Bowerman and his wife often ate waffles for breakfast—not an unusual or special event for them. Yet one morning, while thinking about his shoe designs and eating waffles, Bowerman had a flash of inspiration. He ran into the garage with the waffle iron and poured rubber on it. With that one idea, Bill created Nike's now famous waffle sole. As it turned out, when placed on a lightweight shoe, the waffle sole gripped running tracks better than the established ripple sole. It soon became a major success story. Where did Bowerman's inspiration come from? Was it a random accident or a message from his Inner CEO? I'll let you decide.

When Nike was first started, it did business under the name Blue Ribbon Sports. At one point, the management team decided they needed a new name that would match the new direction they were moving in as they grew bigger. The team was struggling to come up with a new name, and nothing was exciting anyone. One member of the management team, Jeff Johnson, had a dream one night. In the middle of that dream, he got a "flash" that the company should be called Nike, after the winged goddess of victory in Greek mythology. He literally woke up saying, "Nike!"[11] Where did that flash come from, and why did he get it through a dream? The flash came from his Inner CEO, who chose a dream as an effective channel through which to send the message!

Nike had a huge rise to success; then they had some very hard times. The catalyst for their turning things around and experiencing renewed growth came in an interesting way. Nike had always prospered by signing endorsement contracts with athletes. It was a simple exchange where Nike would pay athletes an annual fee, and the athletes would agree to wear Nike's shoes when they played their sport. It was a very effective but indirect form of advertising and promotion. Traditionally, they signed numerous players in various sports and spent a lot of money to do it.

However, during the tough years, they decided to change their strategy away from signing many basketball players in favor of signing one and doing a major push with him. But which player? The player had to be fresh, talented, healthy, charismatic, and fit the Nike image.

There was an ongoing debate about which athlete to pick, and many were considered. But one Nike employee, Sonny Vaccaro, "had a feeling" that it should be Michael Jordan. Given the kind of player Jordan became, that might seem like a no-brainer, but at the time, Michael Jordan was a rookie and not expected by many to go on to do what he did. It was a major gamble for Nike, especially while the company was struggling.

Through tremendous resistance from Jordan, who wanted to sign with Adidas, Nike signed Jordan to a contract, and on his strength, Nike sold $100 million worth of the "Air Jordan" line, saving the company.

Where did Sonny Vaccaro's "feeling" come from? How could he "know" what Jordan would become? Again, you see Inner CEOs at work and information flowing through the invisible network giving unusual insight.

The next example is Dave Thomas, founder of the Wendy's chain. Following is a quote from his autobiography, *Dave's Way*, in which he discusses meeting Colonel Sanders, the founder of Kentucky Fried Chicken: "He introduced himself and asked if I knew him. I pretended I didn't, even though I knew all about him. We sat down over a cup of coffee, and he talked to me like an old friend. I've never met a better salesman. When he left, *I had a sense that this man was going to change my life.*"[12]

Where would he get a "sense" like that?

Dave went on to write, "Kentucky Fried Chicken made it possible for me to meet Kenny King, back in the late 50s, at the Hobby Ranch House. He and a couple of his people came to Fort Wayne to see what Kentucky Fried Chicken was all about. Kenny became my role model for success."[13]

Dave also wrote, "The opening of Wendy's wasn't backed up with any fancy market research, but I had a nose for trends in the restaurant business."[14] Where would somebody get a "nose for trends"—meaning they seem to have information about where things are going? Dave wrote simply, "Back in 1969, these were feelings in my gut. They would have been tough to put into words."[15] Sometimes, that's how we receive the information and the ideas and the response to our requests.

Look at the flow here. Dave meets Colonel Sanders and has a feeling the meeting will change his life. Sanders leads him to Kenny King, who becomes his role model and contributes in major ways to his later success. Dave attributes the success of his business to information coming from "feelings in his gut." You see the patterns at work again—Inner CEOs working through people, ideas, resources, techniques, and strategies!

Colonel Sanders himself received clear help from his Inner CEO in the founding of Kentucky Fried Chicken. From a young age, he was attracted to cooking and loved to cook, spending hours experimenting with various recipes, especially chicken recipes. Where do you think that attraction to cooking chicken came from? A major breakthrough came when a friend of his introduced him to the pressure cooker and encouraged him to use it to continue his experimentation with chicken recipes. Pressure cooking became a key part of the "magic recipe" that launched Kentucky Fried Chicken.

J. Paul Getty, the late oil billionaire, said this in his book *How to Be Rich* about his early days in the oil business when the large oil companies were conspiring to put him out of business:

> The situation could have easily turned into a financial disaster. I decided to make a frontal attack on one of the biggest of all the major oil companies—Shell Oil. By a fortunate coincidence, Sir George Legh-Jones, then the Shell Oil Company's president, happened to be visiting Los Angeles. In desperation, I aimed high,

asked for an interview with him personally, and was informed that he would be happy to see me during his visit. A warm, friendly man, Sir George listened attentively to what I had to say. The deepening scowl that etched across his face as he heard me was all the proof I needed that his firm was not a party to the boycott and that he heartily disapproved of such harsh tactics. When I finished talking, he smiled his reassurance. "Relax," he grinned. "We'll help you."[16]

And they did, which was a huge boost on Getty's road to becoming a billionaire oil tycoon.

Where do you think the idea to request a meeting with Sir George came from? Why do you think Sir George agreed to the meeting? What does "fortunate coincidence" really mean from the perspective of *The 11th Element?* When it has major impact like this, it means the manifestation of time, effort, and planning from your Inner CEO! These are clear examples of Getty's Inner CEO at work, using the invisible network to make things happen to assist him in completing his mission.

Writing in her book *The Hidden Intelligence,* Sandra Weintraub said, "For many executives who rely on intuition, it is likely that their decisions are arrived at by a method similar to that used by Conrad Hilton, who received many intuitive insights in his career: 'I know, when I have a problem and have done all I can—thinking, figuring, planning—I keep listening in a sort of inside silence until something clicks and I feel a right answer.' If it worked for this hotel magnate, why not you?"[17]

Weintraub continued, "Patricia Hambrick is a vice president of global marketing at the Reebok company, based in Massachusetts. Her mission: to drive the brand image in worldwide sales. Hambrick reports directly to Paul Fireman, CEO of Reebok, who encourages his people to tap into their own intuition, whether in the creation of new products, marketing, or internal systems. Hambrick describes Fireman as a great intuitive thinker. 'He has a wonderful feel for the business, encourages and rewards thinking that's out there, and encourages you to trust yourself. In fact, when he bought Reebok, a British company, that decision was almost completely intuitive.'"[18]

Weintraub shares another example from her research: "These are some of the high ideals that prompted Tom Chappell, president of Tom's of Maine. Tom had a strong intuitive feeling that natural toothpaste would sell. Tom's wife and co-owner, Kate Chappell, also seems to know intuitively what flavors of toothpaste will find buyers. Not long ago, she had an idea for making fennel flavored paste and commissioned a market research study on it. The data from the survey suggested that it would be a loser. She disregarded the data, manufactured it anyway, and it has become a winner."[19]

Where do you think Tom's feeling about natural toothpaste came from? Where do you think Kate's knowledge of which flavors would sell came from?

Other examples of Inner CEOs sending information and messages through various channels that resulted in business success include Sony's wildly successful Walkman personal stereo system (where Masoru Ibuka's "gut instinct" told him that a tiny portable tape player would fill a gap of which the consumer was presently unaware), Mrs. Fields' Cookies (when an inner feeling Debbie Fields had caused her to disregard the opinions of her advisors and the results of market research studies to open her first cookie store), Bill and Elsie Sechrist, franchise owners of Budget Rent-A-Car (who received valuable insight and guidance from their Inner CEOs through their dreams), and Elias Howe (whose nightmare about cannibals with spears that had holes at the tips prompted him to have the breakthrough that led to the development of the sewing machine).

Arthur Fry sang in a choir in St. Paul, Minnesota. It bothered him when the bits of paper marking his place in the hymnal kept falling out. One Sunday, he recalled an adhesive a 3M colleague had invented. Unlike most adhesives, this one could be readily detached. Fry's recollection led to the creation of the Post-it notepads, which went on to become one of the five best-selling office products in the world. "'I don't know if it was a dull sermon or divine inspiration,' Fry quipped."[20] Fry's recollection and inspiration are additional examples of Inner CEOs at work!

When his older brother was killed during World War II, Dick Clark withdrew into a shell for a long period. Then he began to listen to the radio to ease his pain. Soon he was dreaming of hosting his own radio show. That led him to start *American Bandstand*, which was the beginning of an extremely successful career for Clark. The influence of Dick's Inner CEO is clear in this example as the true source of his dream.

Napoleon Hill is well-known for his perennial best-selling book *Think and Grow Rich*. The genesis of that book came while Hill was in his early 20s. While working his way through college as a part-time reporter, he accepted an assignment to interview Andrew Carnegie—the wealthiest man in the world at the time. During that interview, Carnegie saw something in Napoleon that intrigued him, which prompted Carnegie to share with Hill the success formula he'd developed over the years, and he invited Hill to organize the formula and make it available to the man on the street. Carnegie opened many doors for Hill and enabled him to have the experiences that led to the best-selling book, a successful career, and great wealth for Hill. Was their meeting accidental or on purpose? And, how and why did Carnegie "see" something in Hill that set everything into motion?

Nathaniel Hawthorne went home to tell his wife that he had just been fired from his job. "Good," she said. "Now you can write your book." "What do we live on meanwhile?" Hawthorne asked. His wife opened a drawer filled with money. "I have always known that you are a man of genius," she said. "So I saved a little each week, and now I have enough to last for a year."[21] Hawthorne used the time to write *The Scarlet Letter*, one of the great masterpieces of American literature. Was this a random accident or the result of their Inner CEOs at work, guided by their life purposes?

Several years ago, there was a best-selling book titled *The Christmas Box*, by Richard Paul Evans. Evans built it into a huge success as a self-published title, and Simon & Schuster paid millions of dollars for the rights to publish the hardcover and audio versions of the book. Evans says he wrote this 87-page Christian-based tale in six weeks and credits a 4:00 A.M. "bolt of divine intervention" with revealing the story to him while he was sitting at his kitchen table.

He wrote, "It really was a miracle, because the story started to write itself. It would just flood into my mind in torrents of inspiration. It would wake me up in the middle of the night. Once, I pulled off the freeway and wrote part of a chapter. I wrote on backs of envelopes, bills, and any scraps of paper I could find in the car."[22] Now you have to ask where did that "bolt" and "inspiration" come from? Might it be a knock-me-over-the-head-so-I-can't-miss-it sign from his Inner CEO to help him fulfill his life purpose and complete part of his mission?

James Redfield wrote a huge best-selling book titled *The Celestine Prophecy* in 1997. Redfield is convinced that some "high power was present" as he wrote and promoted the book. These are his words as he describes the process of writing and selling his novel: "I'm reluctant to say I was chosen," Redfield said, "but I certainly was driven."[23]

J. K. Rowling and the *Harry Potter* series of books and movies give us another excellent example of *The 11th Element* at work. Writing in his book *J. K. Rowling: The Wizard Behind Harry Potter*, Marc Shapiro related the now-famous story of how Rowling got the original idea for the series: "One day, as she returned to London after yet another day of unrewarding work, the train suddenly ground to a halt. There was some kind of a mechanical problem that, it was announced, would require a delay of about four hours. . . . But since Joanne was too tired to either read or write, she focused on a group of cows grazing in a meadow in front of her. What she did not realize was that her life was about to change."[24]

Rowling herself said the following in a "School Library Journal" conversation: "I was sitting on the train just staring out the window at some cows. It was not the most inspiring subject. When all of a sudden, the idea for Harry just appeared in my mind's eye. I can't tell you why or what triggered it, but I saw the idea of Harry and the wizard school very plainly. I suddenly had this basic idea of a boy who didn't know who he was."[25]

Where do you think Rowling got the inspiration? How did the Harry Potter idea appear in her "mind's eye" and why? The answer can be found by looking at her Inner CEO, life purpose, and mission. Again, you see how information and guidance can flow from Inner CEOs in their control rooms.

You will see patterns like these over and over when you start looking at very successful people, the building of their wealth, and the building of successful careers, even if it doesn't involve money.

After J. K. Rowling finished the first *Harry Potter* manuscript, she sent it to two agents in England. One turned her down. The other one, Byrony Evens, took the proposal that was in a black folder and threw it into the trash because the agency didn't do children's books. Ironically, the head of the agency, Christopher Little, didn't think children's books ever made any money. Later that day, however, Evens noticed the unusual black folder in the trash can, and she fished it out to take another look. She loved it and started the project moving.

You have to look at movements like that and ask: Why did Byrony Evens look in the trash can? Why did the folder attract her attention? How did that happen? It happened because the publishing of the *Harry Potter* book had already been planned and arranged from within Rowling's Inner CEO's control room, and it was now in the manifestation phase. All of the involved Inner CEOs, including Byrony's, had to find ways to move things forward together.

If you're interested in seeing more movements like this in the Rowling story, read one of her biographies. The story is really fascinating, especially from the perspective of *The 11th Element.*

Starbucks is one of my favorite success stories because the people who built it are so interesting and because it's such a great illustration of *The 11th Element* at work.

In his book, *Pour Your Heart Into It: How Starbucks Built a Company One Cup at a Time,* Howard Schultz, the current CEO of Starbucks, wrote this: "In 1981, while working for Hammerplast, which was a company that made coffee makers, I noticed a strange phenomenon. A little retailer in Seattle was placing unusually large orders for a certain type of drip coffee maker. It was a simple device, a plastic cone set on a thermos. I investigated. Starbucks Coffee Tea and Spice had only four small stores then. Yet it was buying this product in quantities larger than Macy's. Why should Seattle be so taken with this coffee maker, when the rest of the country was making its daily coffee in electric percolators or drip coffee machines?"[26] What might have caused him to notice that "strange phenomenon"?

Schultz flew out to visit the small Starbucks chain. After he found out what they were doing and why they were buying so many of his coffee makers, he wrote this about his flight back home, "I believe in destiny. In Yiddish, they call it bashert. At that moment, flying 35,000 feet above the earth, I could feel the tug of Starbucks. There was something magic about it; a passion, an authenticity I've never experienced in business. Maybe, just maybe, I could be part of that magic. Maybe I could help it grow."[27] What was the true source of the "tug" he felt?

From that day forward, Schultz tried to go to work for Starbucks so he could become part of the magic he discovered. But Starbucks resisted him. They looked at him as big business and an influence that could destroy their magic. But Schultz persevered, demonstrating perfectly the benefits of persistence when it's aligned with life purpose.

After Schultz went to work for Starbucks and was trying to grow the business, he realized that the genesis of the Starbucks idea came from cafés in Italy. He flew to Italy to experience those cafés firsthand. He became mesmerized by what was happening in Italy in those cafés, and he writes this: "As I watched, I had a revelation. Starbucks had missed the point. Completely missed it. This is so powerful, I thought, this is the link. The connection to the people who loved coffee did not have to take place only in their homes, where they ground and brewed whole-bean coffee. What we had to do was unlock the romance and mystery of coffee, firsthand, in coffee bars. The Italians understood the personal relationship that people could have to coffee; its social aspect. I couldn't believe that Starbucks was in the coffee business, yet was overlooking an element so central to it, like this. It was like an epiphany. It was so immediate and physical that I was shaking."[28]

It was "so immediate and physical," he was "shaking." Does that sound like a knock-me-over-the-head-so-I-can't-miss-it sign? It doesn't get much more obvious than that! Again, observe the patterns being revealed in these success stories.

Here's another great example of the benefits that can come from being open to breakthroughs coming from any direction. For years, Charles Goodyear labored to find a way to make rubber commercially usable. Try as he may, he constantly ran into the proverbial brick wall. Then one day, quite by accident, Goodyear spilled a mixture of rubber and sulfur he was holding onto a hot stove. The chemical reaction of heat applied to this mixture resulted in the discovery of the vulcanization process used to manufacture rubber tires. At that instant, an industry was born, and all of our lives were changed forever.[29]

Goodyear's breakthrough came from a "mistake." Do you think it's possible that his Inner CEO might be the true cause of that "slip"? Remember, help from Inner CEOs—in manifesting responses to requests for help or in fulfilling their own independent projects—can come at any time, in any way.

Lynn Robinson is an author, consultant, and intuitive counselor, who helps entrepreneurs build their businesses by sharing her insights with them. Here's the story of how Lynn's intuitive reading business started:

> I was the operations manager of a small software company. I hated being there, and I dreamed of developing my own business. I had taken classes on developing psychic abilities and found I had a great deal of natural talent in the area. My main concern

was how do I develop a psychic reading business? I quipped that if God posted a psychic reader wanted ad in the *Boston Sunday Globe* employment section, I'd apply. Barring that, I wasn't sure where to begin. I decided to practice my new-found consciousness tools of affirming, visualizing, and asking the universe for help. About a month into this manifesting process, a friend who had been sick for a long time died. As I walked in the room for his funeral service, I felt a strong intuitive inclination to sit next to a woman I hadn't met before. I briefly questioned my reasons for sitting there, as there were quite a few people in the room that I both knew and preferred to sit next to for emotional support. At the end of the service, the woman and I started talking, and she asked me what I did for a living. Have you ever had one of those times when your brain doesn't engage with your mouth? Despite the fact that in my current job I was an operations manager, I answered, "I'm a psychic." I was immediately stricken with alarm. Why had I answered this way? What would she think? I did readings for a few friends and friends of friends, but I never defined my career that way. I felt flustered by my answer. To my surprise, she was quite open and receptive. She then told me that she was a writer for the *Boston Globe* and would love to have a reading, so she could write about it in her column. To make a long story short, she wrote the article, and I had about 400 people call me to schedule an appointment over the next several months. Here's the moral of the story from my perspective: The universe had managed to create a full-time psychic reading business virtually overnight. There is no way I could have created that if I had taken a step-by-step logical approach.[30]

What was the key to Lynn's success? First, getting a feeling to sit next to someone and following that feeling. Notice that if she'd ignored the feeling and sat somewhere else, her Inner CEO would have had to find another way to hook them up or help her. Then she followed another impulse to call herself a psychic. If she'd answered by saying "operations manager," again, her Inner CEO would have had to go to Plan B to hook her up with the reporter or help her build her reading business some other way. This is why you must be open-minded and always on the alert!

Does it excite you to see the movements of *The 11th Element* like this? If you're like me, it almost feels as though you have special x-ray glasses that allow you to see what others can't.

In their book *Hard Drive: Bill Gates and the Making of the Microsoft Empire,* James Wallace and Jim Erickson wrote this about Microsoft cofounders Bill Gates and Paul Allen: "For some time now, they had shared the same vision that one day the computer would be as commonplace in the home as the television set, and that these computers would need software—their software."[31] Here are two people sharing the same vision—not just that there would be computers, not just that the computers would be commonplace, not just that they would need software, but that *they* would be writing the software that would run these computers! If you look at many success stories, you'll see that they also started with a vision. The people having the visions don't necessarily know where they came from, but they started with a vision that grabbed hold of them and wouldn't let go.

Wallace and Erickson also wrote, "Bill Gates undoubtedly cannot explain how he reacted as he did to his own wonder, the computer, when he first discovered it. But it triggered a deep passion, an obsession in him. From that first day in the small computer room in Lakeside High School, its pull on him was inexorable."[32] Where do you think that passion, obsession, and pull came from? Who do you think maintained that pull on Gates to make sure that he moved in that direction, and why? These are the interesting things to think about as you start to live and breathe *The 11th Element.*

The most critical turning point in the early days of Microsoft was when they landed a contract with IBM to build an operating system for the PC that IBM was just about to launch. It was a very secret project. Gates was at a meeting at IBM when they asked him if he could deliver such an operating system. Gates didn't have an operating system like that, but told them he had one and that he'd deliver it bug-free and ready-to-go within a reasonably short time frame. As a result, IBM gave Microsoft the contract.

It later turned out that the exact operating system Gates needed to meet his commitment to IBM had already been written by a computer programmer named Tim Patterson, who lived 20 minutes from Gates in Seattle. Gates bought the operating system from Patterson, and the rest, as they say, is history. Again, the key questions to ask are: Why did Gates feel motivated to promise delivery of an operating system he didn't have? How did he find Tim Patterson and hook up with him to get what he needed? Again, you see Inner CEOs and *The 11th Element* at work.

Robert Kiyosaki has become famous and extremely wealthy through his *Rich Dad, Poor Dad* series of books. If you're not familiar with them, it's a wonderful series that offers a very untraditional approach to managing finances and building wealth.

Kiyosaki originally self-published the first book in the series and could not sell the first print run he had stacked up in his garage. But he felt compelled to continue. One day, a friend of his who owned a car wash suggested that Kiyosaki display the books in his car wash. The friend thought people might see the books on display and buy them while paying their bill or waiting for their cars to be washed.

Kiyosaki put his books on display in the car wash, but only a few sold. One day, however, a guy who was a big shot with a network marketing company happened to be getting his car washed, happened to pick up Kiyosaki's book, loved it, told everybody in his network marketing organization they should buy the book, and also bought many copies himself to give away. One person's visit to a car wash caused sales of Kiyosaki's book to skyrocket and eventually led to Kiyosaki's appearing on Oprah Winfrey's television show. After that, his book became a multimillion-copy bestseller.

What happened there? An Inner CEO was working on the project of getting Kiyosaki's work distributed. The Inner CEO was working on ways to get visibility for the book, to get "the right people" to find their way to it. So, as we discussed in the manifestation step in *The 11th Element* system, due diligence was done, agreements were made, and an action plan was created and executed. It manifested as a friend suggesting Kiyosaki display his books in a car wash and led to Kiyosaki's appearing on the Oprah show, but it all came from his Inner CEO at work! The result? A best-selling book series, tremendous wealth, and millions of people worldwide benefiting from Kiyosaki's unique genius and strategies.

Michael Dell, billionaire founder of Dell, wrote in his book *Direct from Dell:* "By some stroke of luck, the 1982 National Computer Conference was held in June at the Astrodome in Houston four months after I'd gotten my driver's license."[33] Stroke of luck? I think you know better at this point in your *11th Element* education, but attending the show would end up becoming a key moment in the development of his vision and his drive to succeed.

Dell continued in his book, "What I can't say I knew at age 18 was how big the opportunity was. . . . But I did know one thing. I knew what I wanted to do: build better computers than IBM, offer great value and service to the customer by selling direct, and become number one in the industry. Besides my parents, I didn't admit that to anyone, because they probably would have thought I was crazy. But to me, the opportunity was clear."[34] Again, we see a vision and a fortuitous series of events, including a show coming to his city four months after he got his driver's license, all orchestrated by Dell's Inner CEO to help him fulfill his life purpose and complete his mission.

Dell also wrote, "I knew in my heart that I was onto a fabulous business opportunity that I could not let pass me by."[35] He added, "And I felt that this was absolutely the right time to go for it. . . . As it turned out, the timing for PCs Limited [the original name for his company] couldn't have been better."[36] Where do you think that his "knowing" and his "feeling" came from? And how do you think his timing ended up being so perfect?

My friend Bob Sterling shared another story that clearly illustrates *The 11th Element* at work:

This example has been worth millions to me in business. Nearly 10 years ago, I met a professor from UCLA at an alumni event. During our conversation, I discovered that he had developed a unique testing technology that was used primarily for primary education. I realized it had tremendous value for the corporate world and asked him if he would be willing to let me market it to large corporations. He agreed, but we subsequently discovered there were too many technical restrictions to make it practical for business use. So I stored the concept away in my brain with the strong instinct that it would someday prove valuable. Nine years later, knowing that I'm a product developer, a friend asked me if I had any ideas for a business that could be done over the Internet, that would generate millions in annual sales. I told him I'd get back to him. That night, I awoke at 3:00 with a brainstorm. Using the power of the Internet, I could tweak the professor's technology to remove the major stumbling blocks that were a problem in the earlier version. After confirming that this would work with the professor, the three of us agreed to go into business together and make the technology available to large corporations. In just 17 months, we built the software, signed up a number of blue chip customers, and sold the business for $6.25 million. Another hunch had paid off far better than I'd ever imagined.[37]

One last story before we move on comes to me from a friend, Bill Harris, owner of the Centerpointe Research Institute in Oregon. His company sells a very powerful meditation program. Bill wrote this to me when I asked for examples of *The 11th Element* principles at work in the building of his successful business:

One of the most amazing things I've found in my success has been the ability to tap into the answer for any question I need answered, just by continually asking it. For this reason, I find I can undertake and successfully accomplish any project or endeavor without knowing in advance how I'm going to bring it to the finish line. I just ask, "How am I going to get more people to buy my product, or how can I raise the money I need for this, or how can I get more visitors to my web site to actually buy my product," or any other question. As far as I'm concerned, the more difficult and outrageous the question, the more fun the challenge is. I find that focusing on the question always brings the answer to me. Either it pops into my head, or a book pops off the shelf at the bookstore, or I meet someone who has the answer, or I overhear a snatch of a conversation in a crowd from someone who knows the answer, or it comes to me in some other way—often one I would never have anticipated. What I need to know appears. It's the most amazing thing. But I have come to rely on this phenomenon to such a degree that I never worry any more about how I will find an answer. No matter how tough the problem, I just know that if I continually focus on the question, the answer will come. Some unseen force always sends the answer if you put out the call and just keep asking. Using this method, I've been able to build my business from $12,000 in annual sales in 1990 to over $4.6 million in 2001. My goal is $35 million annually, and I have no doubt I will reach it.[38]

Can you see how Bill has been getting requests for help onto the desk of his Inner CEO and has been alert enough to receive the help when it came?

I've shared many stories with you in this chapter. But there are so many more. You can go into any library or bookstore, pick up a book about any wealth-building story, whether it's about an entrepreneur, athlete, actor, or media personality, and you'll see the same patterns, the same *11th Element* principles at work. You can pick up books about people who've been successful, not from the wealth they've created, but because they're contributing valuable information to others; people who are terrific parents, terrific teachers, terrific healers, and so on; and you'll see the same patterns, the same *11th Element* principles at work.

Marlo Thomas wrote a book titled *The Right Words at the Right Time*.[39] The book contains stories about people who became very successful in various fields. In each story, the people share the one thing they considered the absolute key to their success, and it was always something someone said to them at a particular time that just swooped in and had huge impact on what they were trying to produce. The book is particularly interesting from the perspective of *The 11th Element* because you will see Inner CEOs at work in numerous ways—using people, ideas, resources, techniques, and strategies as their raw material to help us succeed.

Once you begin applying *The 11th Element* system, you have to be on the lookout for these kinds of movements in your life. You must be patient and take the time to work with your Inner CEO to nail down your code systems and the knock-me-over-the-head signs that will fuel your success.

In short, when your requests are approved, events will be set in motion. You must then be sensitive to the movement and on the lookout for clues, signals, guidance, and opportunities—even if they defy logic or contradict what the experts and your advisors say.

Is Anything Flying beneath the Radar?

If someone is going down the wrong road, he doesn't need motivation to speed him up. What he needs is education to turn him around.[1]

—Jim Rohn

When you interact with customers, employees, suppliers, and other business contacts in person, on the phone, through sales letters, advertisements, e-mails, or any other medium, there are actually two kinds of messages being communicated:

- On the surface (what everyone can see and hear)
- Through the master biography files stored in the invisible network

As you recall from Chapter 1, the label *master biography file* describes all the up-to-date information stored about you and your activities in the invisible network search engines. Master biography files are very thorough and complete. If you have fears, they're stored in your master biography files. If you're really good at something, that information is stored in your master biography files. If you have weaknesses, that information is stored in the master biography files. Your wishes, dreams, wants, and needs are stored in your master biography files. Everything you're thinking and feeling at any given moment flows into the master biography files. All the details about your business and wealth-building activities are stored in your master biography files.

Nothing is missing, hidden, secret, or sugar-coated. Where Inner CEOs live and work, and at the level where the invisible network operates, we're all open books. Information is being added to your master biography files, and the files are being updated and revised on a real-time basis 24 hours a day, 7 days a week. This process has been running since you were born and will continue until you die.

Although you may have work to do in various areas, when the information on the surface matches the information in the master biography files, your business has the raw potential to succeed and prosper. If the information on the surface says one thing, but the master biography files say something else, the resulting mismatch can cause serious problems: lost sales, customer satisfaction issues, employee morale and retention problems, refund problems, productivity decreases, outright business failure, and so on. Mismatches don't always have negative or limiting impact on you, but because they can, you should be vigilant about coordinating the information on the surface with the master biography file information in the invisible network (see Figure 7.1).

In addition, if there's a large amount of positive information about you or your efforts in your master biography files, that information will support your efforts and help you. Conversely, if there's a large amount of negative information about you and your efforts in the master biography files, like mismatches, it can cause serious damage.

FIGURE 7.1 When the content of your master biography files and surface communication matches, tremendous power is instantly available to you.

Radar is used by the military and air traffic controllers to detect and track the movements of aircraft and other flying objects and as an early warning system of possible danger. Although radar is a very effective tool, it's possible to fly beneath the radar or use stealth technology to go undetected and cause damage. In such cases, other technologies must be used as needed to detect and neutralize such movements.

Similarly, as you work to build a successful business and wealth, you'll use your own kind of radar to detect and track anything that might block your progress or be dangerous to you. But the information stored in master biography files can easily fly under your radar, go undetected, and cause damage to your efforts. Because master biography files are taken literally (like everything else in the invisible network), you must manage them on an ongoing basis and employ other technologies as needed to detect and neutralize them.

Recall the example in Chapter 1 in which you might meet somebody for the first time and instantly like them, trust them, and feel comfortable with them. Or, you don't like them, don't trust them, or don't feel comfortable with them. In these situations, you're picking up a match or a mismatch between who you are and who they are, what you want and what they want, or what they're saying and doing and the contents of their master biography files. The important fact to recognize, however, is that when you have such feelings, you're actually tapping into the master biography files, either on your own or by getting information from your Inner CEO, the content is having impact, and a similar process affects the buying patterns of people worldwide.

Managing the contents of your master biography files involves *regularly* performing three tasks:

1. Resolving mismatches before they can have impact.
2. Proactively seeking to have positive and empowering entries added to your files.
3. Uncovering the entries or mismatches that are currently having negative impact and editing or neutralizing them.

Resolving Mismatches before They Can Have Impact

Any time there's a mismatch between what's stored in the master biography files and what's happening on the surface in your daily life, there can be problems. And the problems can be huge.

For example, suppose you needed to buy a new mattress, and you found an ad in your local newspaper that began with this:

"Come to our store to buy your next mattress. Our mattresses are chiropractor and doctor approved to give your back the best possible support. They have the longest and best warranties on the market and will last forever. We absolutely offer the best overall bang-for-the-buck value on the market. We even deliver and set everything up for free." Further suppose, however, that at the end of the ad there was a postscript that said, "By the way, the mattresses we currently have in stock got wet when our roof leaked last week, and although we dried them out, they're not up to our usual quality standards." If you were reading a postscript like that, even if you were positively predisposed to buy before reading it, you'd probably change your mind because the statement was so powerful and damaging that it would undercut everything else you read.

As silly or unrealistic as that example might seem, similar types of mismatches occur in business on a daily basis—as a result of what salespeople say or what businesses communicate through their ads, sales letters, brochures, flyers, web sites, in-person exchanges, phone conversations, and so on.

The postscript in this ad is the equivalent of a master biography file entry. Many people sense those mismatches, decide not to buy, or delay their decisions as a result—often without being aware of it or knowing why.

Until now, you may have believed the only thing affecting the results you produced was what was communicated at the surface level that everyone can see and hear. But now you know that master biography files exist, and that mismatches can be created that have major negative or limiting impact on your efforts. As a result, you need to be very careful not to create mismatches (especially in sales and marketing where it's so tempting and easy for things to get hyped or exaggerated, where too much glitz or sizzle can be added, and so on). And if mismatches are created unintentionally, you need to resolve them quickly, before they can have impact.

As obvious as it sounds, the best strategy for preventing mismatches from occurring in the first place is to be direct and honest at all times. The best way to do this is to follow this simple rule:

Live your daily life as if everything you're thinking, everything you're feeling, and every entry in your master biography files are being picked up *consciously* by everyone you're interacting with. This rule applies in my life whether someone is reading a sales letter from me, visiting my web site, reading an ad I have in a magazine, talking to me on the phone, attending a seminar, or receiving any other form of communication from me or my company. I begin with that rule in mind; then I say to myself, "If the other people or person actually knew all that, what, if anything, would I say or do differently to change things?" Then, if there's a mismatch of any kind, I take the appropriate action to resolve the mismatch—either on my own or by asking my Inner CEO for help.

If you find yourself interacting with another person—face to face or through some other sales, marketing, or corporate communication channel—and you're saying one thing but thinking another, or you know something you said wasn't true or wasn't completely true, or you're withholding some piece of potentially impactive information, you should instantly catch yourself and say, "All right, there's a potential mismatch here. How can I fix it?"

You may be wondering, "Well, if this is true, how do so many dishonest or unethical people succeed and prosper? Why don't the mismatches block or hurt them?" The answer to that is complicated. In some cases, it does hurt and block them, and they ultimately fail. You can see examples of this every day in the business headlines and news. In other cases, some people are more sensitive than others, and not everyone consciously picks up on mismatches, although they could start to if they asked their Inner CEOs to help them become more sensitive. In other cases, even if it seems hard to believe, it is often part of someone's mission or life purpose to be cheated or misled by such people. That has happened to me many times, and the lessons I learned from the experiences helped me in important ways afterward. Frequently, the persons being dishonest or unethical are exploring the impact of such behavior as part of their life purpose and mission, and others at the unconscious level agree to support them in their exploration. There are many possible explanations, but unless you feel that your mission is to explore such possibilities and realities, you would be wise to manage your master biography file content as carefully, honestly, and ethically as possible.

Proactively Seeking to Have Positive and Empowering Entries Added to Your Files

There's tremendous opportunity every day to consciously and intentionally place positive entries into your master biography files. To do that, you must ask yourself a series of what I call *core issue* questions, such as:

- Why does my business exist?
- Why was it formed?
- What need or want does it genuinely fulfill?
- What core beliefs and ideas drive my efforts?
- What am I trying to do through the business for myself and others, and why?
- How can I better serve my prospects, customers, vendors, or partners?
- How can I get even better at what I do?

Make sure you're very clear on core issues such as these.

If you're not clear on why you're *really* doing what you're doing or what you're planning to do, if you're not really clear on what you want to get through your business and wealth-building efforts, your master biography file entries might not be as compelling as a competitor's, and your sales, profits, and progress will suffer as a result.

For example, suppose you've decided to buy a product to solve a problem, and you're considering two companies from which to buy. Suppose the price and basic product package are the same. Suppose you're talking to one business owner who has entries in his master biography files such as: "This product is fantastic, and you're absolutely going to receive X, Y, and Z benefits. But do you know what? This is the real world. Things can go wrong with any product. Things can break. You can spill hot coffee on it. There can be problems. I want you to know that if anything goes wrong, you have my home phone number, you have my e-mail and pager, you can call me 24 hours a day, 7 days a week. I'm going to be there to help you because I believe in this product and in helping my customers. I've been in this business for 23 years because I love it. I want to actually solve the problem you're coming to us to solve. That's who I am and what I'm all about."

Suppose another business owner has entries in his master biography files such as: "It's a good product. It does the job. And I want you to buy the product because I need the income. I'm behind on my rent, utilities, and copier lease payment."

Now, there's nothing wrong with the second business owner being behind on his bills. I've been there myself. But the question is: Do such master biography file entries have impact? Of course. If you consciously read the master biography file entries of the two business owners, which one would you want to buy from? If you're like most of the people I speak with, it would be the first one because the content of the first master biography file is so much more inviting. You want the same thing to be true for your master biography files. As you'll see in the next chapter, there are exceptions, but the most successful people and companies tend to have the most compelling master biography files.

So, on a daily basis, by simply committing yourself to doing the best job you can do; by remaining clear on your motives, preferences, and comfort zone; and by looking for ways to genuinely serve your prospects and customers better, you can proactively insert positive entries into your master biography files that will serve you in major ways going forward. You can also proactively impact the content of your master biography files by simply asking your Inner CEO to help you make the changes that will lead to more positive entries being stored in your master biography files.

Uncovering the Entries or Mismatches That Are Currently Having Negative Impact and Editing or Neutralizing Them

Mine fields are very dangerous. Mines sit there silent and innocent-looking, but you're in serious trouble if you ever hit one. Likewise, you can be zooming in your spaceship toward your chosen destination and everything may seem fine; but then you hear a thud, there's an explosion, and before you know it, major damage has been done to your ship. It doesn't matter how good a pilot you are, how important your mission is, how good a map or plan you have, or how skilled your crew is—if you hit a mine, major damage results.

Negative master biography file entries or mismatches (negative files) are like mines. You're zooming along on the way to your ideal outcome, thinking you're making great progress. Then suddenly you hear the thud, and before you know it, the negative file "mine" explodes, and you're blown off course. And, in most cases, you didn't know the files or mismatches even existed, much less that they were active and dangerous.

Examples of negative files at work include hidden problems with your product or service, low employee morale, financial struggles, confusion or lack of clarity about your company mission, lawsuits against you from disgruntled employees or customers, dishonesty in your advertising or marketing messages, illegal business practices, and so on.

If you know where the mines are in a mine field, you can neutralize each one separately, then fly through the field unencumbered and without worry. Similarly, because negative files can be so powerful and so damaging, it is important to have techniques and strategies for uncovering and neutralizing them. Many such techniques and strategies are offered in Appendix B of this book.

We continue our discussion of master biography files and how to proactively work with them to your benefit in the next chapter.

Going beyond Salespeople, Marketing, and Word of Mouth

There are no unimportant people.[1]
—Aaron Scheinfeld

Coming together is a beginning; keeping together is progress; working together is success.[2]

—Henry Ford

When working to increase sales and profits, most business owners focus on increasing the effectiveness of salespeople, marketing, and word of mouth. Those are powerful and wise strategies, and, as I hope you're beginning to see, if you want

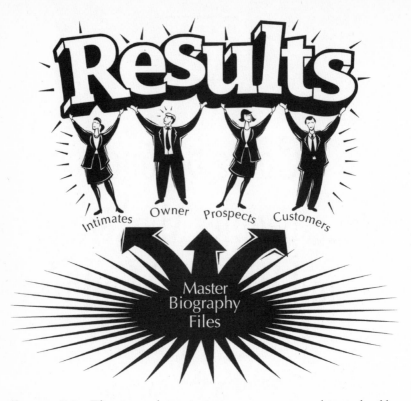

FIGURE 8.1   The group dynamic impacts your master biography files and the results you produce in powerful and amazing ways.

to go beyond what's possible with such surface-based strategies (no matter how effective they may be), you must focus your energy on master biography file entries. In this chapter, we discuss additional ways to do that.

   If you're going to build a successful business and create wealth, you'll need help from many other people (employees, prospects, customers, vendors), and the resulting group dynamic will impact your master biography file entries and the results you produce in powerful ways (see Figure 8.1). Master biography file entries from the following groups will have the most impact:

- Employees, vendors, contractors, and others who are intimately involved with your business (your intimates)
- Prospects and customers

Intimates

All your intimates have Inner CEOs. They each have a unique mission and life purpose they came here to fulfill. They each have the ability to work with their Inner CEO to get help with the tasks that impact your business, if they are properly motivated to do so. In addition, they each have the ability to limit their potential (and yours) if they're not properly motivated or if they're unhappy.

Your intimates have chosen to merge their missions and life purposes with yours, either briefly or in a long-term sense (depending on how entwined you are); but they still have their own agendas at the core level, and you have to take that into consideration as you look at ways to motivate, reward, manage, and treat them.

All of your intimates have thoughts, feelings, and opinions about their jobs or roles, your company, your products and services, your management team, other employees, the way you run your business, how they're being treated by you or other people in your company, the way you treat your prospects and customers, what your prospects and customers think about your business, and more. All of those thoughts, feelings, and opinions get added into the master biography files on your business and can have a major impact on the success of your business—either positive or negative. It's critical to understand this.

The most successful entrepreneurs are those who are able to attract or create intimates who support their efforts from the perspective of *The 11th Element*. They're able to structure their businesses and strategies so that all intimates are educated to understand and inspired to align with the corporate mission, goals, culture, guiding values, and principles. As a result, the master biography files on their companies are enhanced, not diminished, by their intimates.

The most successful entrepreneurs are also masters at motivating intimates to tap into *The 11th Element* to maximize their own personal productivity and the quality of the results they produce in their specific roles. You can send requests to your Inner CEO asking for help to improve the productivity of your intimates (which is a wise thing to do), but that's not as powerful as motivating your intimates to do it themselves. As you've seen, it's possible to tap into *The 11th Element* without meaning to or intending to, but when the system is used consciously and proactively, so much more power is available. Therefore, sharing this material with your intimates is another wise move.

When all (or the majority) of your intimates are sending supportive and positive entries into the master biography files, when your intimates are aligned with and believe in your mission, and when your intimates are all consciously and proactively working with their Inner CEOs to enhance their own productivity, the amount of power available to you is staggering. Later in the chapter are many examples of the kind of results this alignment makes possible.

There's another component to consider. My grandfather used to tell me: "In business, there are idea men, implementers, and the rare few who can do both well. To succeed, a company, particularly in the executive ranks, must be balanced with both skill sets." This statement may make sense to you already from the surface level, but let's look at it from the perspective of *The 11th Element*.

As we've discussed, success requires people, ideas, resources, techniques, and strategies. If your company is balanced with idea people and implementers, requests for help are going to Inner CEOs for everything you need. If your company has too many idea people and not enough implementers, however, relatively few requests for help will be sent for techniques, strategies, and other implementation needs. Conversely, if your company has too many implementers and not enough idea people, too few requests for ideas will be sent. In both scenarios, results can suffer.

Manpower, Inc., is a great example of the benefits associated with a top management team being balanced. My grandfather (chairman of the board) was an idea man who could also implement, Elmer Winter (president) was an idea man, and my father (executive vice president) was an implementer. Dell and Starbucks are other excellent examples. You can look closely at virtually any consistently successful business partnership or management team, and you'll see the *balanced dynamic* in operation. Lack of a balanced dynamic is often the reason many entrepreneurs fail, or they may succeed for a while and then fail after the business begins to grow.

As a result, be sure to look at the structure of your business affairs and ask for help to create the balanced dynamic if it's not already in place. This becomes even more important if you're a one-man band, because the likelihood is that you will be strong in only one of the components and must somehow balance yourself out.

Prospects and Customers

A very successful strategy in sales and marketing is using customer testimonials where satisfied customers rave about your business in print, audio, or video formats. Remember, however, that all your prospects and customers have the ability to add entries to your master biography files. If your master biography files are jam-packed with positive testimonials about your company, the impact can be enormous. Similarly, if your master biography files are jam-packed with complaints, your results will suffer (short term or long term).

My sister, Shaina Noll, created a very successful business selling CDs of her own music. Her current titles, which may be familiar to you, include *Songs for the Inner Child, Bread for the Journey,* and *You Can Relax Now.* Each of the titles is designed to nourish and support people emotionally at very deep levels. Her business has become extremely successful, yet she has no salespeople, and she has never spent a dime on marketing or advertising. How did she manage that? Because the master biography files on her music business are so jam-packed with rave reviews from customers that they caught the attention of many Inner CEOs, who spread the word through the invisible network. Thousands of people found their way to her music, and more are finding it daily.

The *Harry Potter* books could be labeled a *phenomenon;* that is, the books seemed to take on a life of their own, and they took the world by storm. Millions of people loved them and spread the word worldwide: "You've *got* to read this book." Sales started out slowly and then exploded. What caused the explosion? Tremendously positive master biography file entries that literally surged through the invisible network with excitement and urging to get the books.

Similar phenomena have occurred with other books, movies, clothing, shoes, and other products and services. I'm sure you're aware of many from your own experience. Two fantastic books were written about the surface causes of such phenomena: *The Tipping Point,*[3] by Malcolm Gladwell, and *Anatomy of Buzz,*[4] by Emanuel Rosen. Both books are fascinating in their own right but when looked at through your new *11th Element* eyes, they're even more rewarding, and you'll see wonderful examples of *The 11th Element* principles at work.

The more I work with clients and *The 11th Element* principles, the more convinced I become that all sales and marketing really do is open doorways that invisible network activity and Inner CEOs then guide people through.

Examples of How Master Biography Files Influence Business Success

We now take a closer look at how master biography file entries by intimates, prospects, and customers translate into tangible, take-it-to-the-bank results. When I first began working with Blue Ocean Software, what impressed me most was what I called their *raw material.* Our product was help desk software, which was in great demand in the information technology community. But more importantly, our customers loved us and gushed about how great our product (Track-It!) was and how much they enjoyed doing business with us.

Do you think master biography file entries like that contributed to our success? Absolutely. On top of glowing customer testimonials in the master biography files, there was also a passion for the company mission, strong loyalty to the company, and a tremendous commitment from each employee to operate at the highest possible level of efficiency and productivity. There was also an unusually strong commitment and focus by our CEO on doubling sales (or better) every year while generating profits of 50 percent or better. That commitment and focus motivated our intimates in their daily work and shaped many of the things we did every day. We prided ourselves on having as much or more revenue per employee as Microsoft, which is generally regarded as the most successful software company in the world.

During the five years I worked with Blue Ocean Software, we broke sales record after sales record, profit record after profit record, and we had consistently better months and quarters. But we did stumble twice during that period. In both cases, the stumble occurred after major new entries were sent into our master biography files. The first stumble came just after a venture capital (VC) firm invested in the company. The minute we joined forces, the voice and agenda of the VC were added to our master biography files. In addition, because the VC was now part owner of the company, it began making demands and exerting pressure to change how we did things. The tension that resulted caused a temporary loss of focus, which impacted our master biography files in negative ways, too. These two factors caused our results to suffer temporarily. We quickly recovered from that stumble, however, and went on to produce even stronger results.

The second stumble occurred for similar reasons after Intuit acquired the company. As the new owner of the company, Intuit exerted pressure to change many things at Blue Ocean. This resulted in many changes to master biography file entries, further loss of focus, and, for some people, a loss of motivation and excitement.

Intuit had its own master biography files merging with Blue Ocean's, which resulted in still more changes. In addition, during the years of tremendous growth and profitability leading up to the acquisition, Blue Ocean was driven by *renegade energy*. We prided ourselves on doing things very differently from other companies. That renegade energy was created and sustained by several people, including me. After the acquisition, the renegades either left the company, as I did, or found it difficult to retain the same passion, focus, and drive. Further, new people who did not share the same renegade attitude and approach were brought into the company. These changes among the intimates of Blue Ocean impacted the master biography file entries (and results) in major ways, and they were perhaps the most damaging changes of all. At the time of this writing, it's too soon to say whether Blue Ocean will recover from that stumble, and if so, how long it will take. Completely new master biography files and intimates are now driving the company.

Remember that any change in a company also changes the master biography file entries about the company. The bigger the change, the greater the impact, and the greater potential for the results to change—for better or worse.

Other than Blue Ocean Software, the biggest corporate success story I have participated in was the company Connecting Point of America. To this day, I've never witnessed *The 11th Element* master biography file management strategies executed better than they were executed at Connecting Point.

The mission of the company was crystal clear: to become a dominant player in the computer franchise business and to do it by giving franchisees what they really wanted (versus what the franchisor felt like giving them). At the time, most franchised computer stores disliked their franchisors and felt that they gave away too much of their profit for too little benefit. However, they were bound by iron-clad 10- to 15-year contracts and could not leave the franchises. Because of the widespread disenchantment and unfavorable contract terms, many independent computer store owners chose to remain independent, even though they would have enjoyed some of the benefits of being franchised. There was an enormous opportunity to enter the computer franchise store niche, serve the community better, and do it in a way that really was a gigantic win-win for *everyone* (not just the franchisor).

So, the Connecting Point management team decided, "We're going to turn the computer franchise industry on its ear by creating a revolutionary new program that gives computer store owners what they've been screaming for but haven't been able to get." There was tremendous passion about that mission. It started with the Connecting Point CEO, a magical man named Mark Shumate (who's still one of my business heroes), and flowed down through every intimate. Everyone was inspired by the mission to serve the franchisees as best as they possibly could.

But there was one aspect of that "fire" that worked absolute magic within the invisible network. Because most computer store franchisors had a 10- to 15-year contract that could not be broken, many franchisees went to court, sued their franchisors trying to get out of the contracts, and failed. Connecting Point decided to offer a 60-day out clause in their contract, which meant that at any point, all franchisees had to do was give 60 days' notice and they were out.

Now, the 60-day out clause had two kinds of magic. The obvious magic was that if a computer store owner was considering joining us, it was a much easier decision because he or she could say, "Hey, if this doesn't work out, I'm not stuck for 10 to 15 years. I can get out quickly and easily." But the real magic came from another direction. Before I left the company, we had approximately 2,500 franchisees, all of whom could leave with 60 days' notice if we didn't treat them well or give them the best possible pricing and the best possible products, services, and a steady stream of other goodies they needed to succeed and prosper. That awareness on the part of the employees and management team increased our already strong desire to serve our customers because if we ceased to do so, all the franchisees would leave, and the whole business would crumble.

Shumate and the management team didn't stop there, however. They recognized that the success of Connecting Point was directly tied to how well the employees did their jobs, so they offered a very generous benefits program that made employees feel valued and appreciated. They also devised a brilliant, extremely lucrative, multi-level, company-wide financial bonus and incentive program that added even more motivation for each employee to embrace the mission and excel in a specific role.

The new computer store franchise program launched with this foundation revolutionized the industry and caught on like wildfire. The computer store owners loved us and loved how we helped them grow their sales and profits. As a result, the franchise development team I was part of added more franchisees in an average week than most of our competitors added in an entire year. We were growing so fast we could barely keep up with it, and our own sales and profits were soaring.

If you looked at the master biography files for Connecting Point, you saw a revolutionary win-win program that delivered tremendous benefits to the franchisees. You saw that all employees were motivated to perform their duties to the best of their abilities. You saw the genuine commitment to serve, which was part of the culture, and you saw the enhanced commitment to serve that was created by the 60-day out clause. And you saw thousands of rave review testimonials about the company from intimates and satisfied franchisees. The result? Growth from $90 million to $350 million over a three-year period, a buyout of the company by a billion-dollar competitor, and a huge financial windfall for the management team and several key intimates.

Michael Dell wrote this about the Dell environment: "We challenged ourselves constantly, to grow more or to provide better service to our customers, and each time we set a new goal, we would make it. Then we'd stop for a moment, give each other a few high fives, and get started on tackling the next goal. People seemed to be energized by being around colleagues who had high expectations of themselves and the company. The first day we did $1 million in sales, someone brought in cupcakes with '$1,000,000' written on each one. We tried to make it so that working at Dell wasn't just somewhere to spend time and collect a paycheck; it was fun, and often, an adventure."[5]

Dell continued:

> We learned to identify our core strengths. Pretty early on in the company's life, we concluded that we wanted to earn a reputation for providing great customer service, as well as great products. The idea was that building a business solely on price was not a sustainable advantage. There would always be someone with something that was lower in price or cheaper to produce. What was really important was sustaining loyalty among customers and employees, and that could only be derived from having the highest level of service and very high-performing products. We put a great deal of emphasis on understanding what drove customer satisfaction, whether it was response times on the telephone, quality of products, valuable features, or the ease of experience in using the product. Engaging the entire company—from manufacturing to engineering to sales to support staff—in the process of understanding customer requirements because a constant focus of management energy, training, and employee education. We learned the importance of ignoring conventional wisdom and doing things our way.[6]

Can you see how intentions, focus, and master biography files like that contributed in major ways to the success of Dell—and how their files stood out from the crowd?

Howard Schultz, CEO of Starbucks, wrote this, "Whatever your cultures, your values, your guiding principles, you have to take steps to inculcate them in the organization early in its life so that they can guide every decision, every hire, every strategic objective you set. Whether you are CEO or a lower-level employee, the single most important thing you do at work each day is communicate your values to others, especially new hires. Establishing the right tone at the inception of an enterprise, whatever its size, is vital to its long-term success."[7]

If you've studied leadership or management, you've heard comments like Schultz's before. But now you can look at this wisdom from the perspective of master biography files and see the kind of impact they can have in positive and negative ways.

Schultz continued, "We built the Starbucks brand first with our people, not with the consumers—the opposite approach from that of the crackers-and-cereal companies. Because we believed the best way to meet and exceed the expectations of customers was to hire and train great people, we invested in employees who were zealous about good coffee. Their passion and commitment made our retail partners our best ambassadors for the coffee and for the brand. Their knowledge and fervor created a buzz among customers and inspired them to come back. That's the secret of the power of Starbucks brand: the personal attachment our partners feel and the connection they make with our customers."[8]

Can you see the power of what Schultz did from the perspective of master biography files? What do you think a "buzz" among customers really means? It means messages flying through the invisible network, shoring up the Starbucks master biography files with very positive entries.

Schultz continued, "In this ever-changing society, the most powerful and enduring brands are built from the heart. They are real and sustainable. Their foundations are stronger because they are built with the strength of the human spirit, not an ad campaign. The companies that are lasting are those that are authentic."[9] *Authentic* means the master biography file entries are clear, clean, inspiring, compelling, and they're totally in alignment with the company mission and daily activities.

Schultz also wrote:

At Starbucks, our product is not just great coffee but also what we call the "Starbucks experience": an inviting, enriching environment in our stores that is comfortable and accessible yet also stylish and elegant. More and more, I realize, customers are looking for a Third Place, an inviting, stimulating, sometimes even soulful respite from the pressures of work and home. People come to Starbucks for a refreshing time-out, a break in their busy days, a personal treat. Their visit has to be rewarding. If any detail is wrong, the brand suffers. That's why we love the saying, "Everything matters." In effect, our stores are our billboards. Customers form an impression of the Starbucks brand the minute they walk in the door. The ambience we create there has as much to do with brand-building as the quality of the coffee. Every Starbucks store is carefully designed to enhance the quality of everything the customers see, touch, hear, smell, or taste. All the sensory signals have to appeal to the same high standards. The artwork, the music, the aromas, the surfaces all have to send the same subliminal message as the flavor of the coffee: *Everything here is best-of-class.*[10]

How do you begin to experience something the minute you walk in a door somewhere? Certainly what you experience on the surface with your five senses contributes, but the real impact comes from master biography files that are so strong you can feel them when you walk in. What do you think ambience really is? Where do you think it comes from? It comes primarily from powerful entries in master biography files.

Schultz went on to say:

If there's one accomplishment I'm proudest of at Starbucks, it's the relationship of trust and confidence we've built with the people who work at the company. That's not just an empty phrase, as it is at so many companies. We've built it into such groundbreaking programs as a comprehensive health-care program, even for part-timers, and stock options that provide ownership for everyone. We treat warehouse workers and entry-level retail people with the kind of respect most companies show for only high executives. These policies and attitudes run counter to conventional business wisdom. A company that is managed only for the benefit of shareholders treats its employees as a line item, a cost to be contained. Executives who cut jobs aggressively are often rewarded with a temporary run-up in their stock price. But in the long run, they are not only undermining morale but sacrificing the innovation, the entrepreneurial spirit, and the heartfelt commitment of the very people who could elevate the company to greater heights. What many in business don't realize is that it's a not a zero-sum game. Treating employees benevolently shouldn't be viewed as an added cost that cuts into profits, but as a powerful energizer that can grow the enterprise into something far greater than one leader could envision. With pride in their work, Starbucks people are less likely to leave. Our turnover rate is less than half the industry average, which not only saves money but strengthens our bond with customers. But the benefits run even deeper. If people relate to the company they work for, if they form an emotional tie to it and buy into its dreams, they will pour their heart into making it better. When employees have self-esteem and self-respect, they can contribute so much more: to their company, to their family, to the world.[11]

Can you see how that philosophy impacted the Starbucks employees and their motivation to excel in their individual roles? Can you see how it led to massively positive entries in the Starbucks master biography files that contributed in *huge* ways to the success and dominance of the company? With what you now know about *The 11th Element,* does it surprise you that Starbucks is so successful—with conscious intentions and master biography files like this?

In every Marriott hotel, there's a copy of a book in the bedside table drawer titled *The Spirit to Serve, Marriott's Way.* The foreword to that book was written by Jim Collins, author of *Built to Last: Successful Habits of Visionary Companies* and *Good to Great: Why Some Companies Make the Leap . . . and Others Don't.* Collins wrote this about the Marriott organization: "Truly great companies maintain a set of core values and a core mission that remains fixed, while their business strategies and practices continually adapt to a changing world. Similarly, the company's core purpose to make people away from home feel that they are among friends and are really wanted serves as a fixed point of guidance and inspiration. Great companies generate substantial wealth, but great companies do not let the pursuit of profit divert them from their central purpose."[12]

How do you think having a core mission of helping people away from home feel that they are among friends and are really wanted impacts the master biography files for Marriott? How do you think it impacts how they train their intimates, what the intimates do on a daily basis, how they do it, what kinds of entries the intimates make in the master biography files, and how guests feel when in the hotels?

Collins added, "As Mr. Marriott writes in these pages, the company has gone astray when it has lost sight of its basic purpose."[13] And he concluded by saying, "For the key to prospering and adapting in the coming decades, amidst an ever-escalating rate of change, is to first be clear about and resolutely dedicated to what you stand for and why that should never change. You must then be just as resolutely willing to change absolutely everything else. The rare ability to manage continuity and change is the secret of Marriott's past and the key to its future."[14]

When you lose sight of your basic purpose, what happens to your master biography file entries? And what does that do to results? Are the patterns and *The 11th Element* truths starting to get even clearer to you? To maximize the results produced and the benefits received, the process of building successful businesses and wealth must involve going beyond salespeople, marketing, and word of mouth to include the conscious and astute management of intimates and master biography files.

Use the techniques, strategies, and insights you gained in this and the previous chapter, and work with your Inner CEO to ensure that your master biography file entries are as positive, powerful, compelling, and authentic as possible.

Author's note: I'm always testing, developing, and adapting new techniques and resources to help uncover and process master biography file entries. To get on my mailing list so you can stay up-to-date, visit this page on my web site: http://www.11thelement.com/mbf.html.

Knowing When to Hold or Fold Your Hand

The universe is full of magical things patiently waiting for our wits to grow sharper.[1]

—Eden Phillpotts

Accept the challenges, so that you may feel the exhilaration of victory.[2]

—General George S. Patton

When playing poker, despite the actual cards you're holding and the apparent strength or weakness of your hand, there are times when you *hold* (stay in the game) and times when you *fold* (quit that hand because it serves your best long-term interests to start over with a new hand). You make the decision based on the available information (including intuition or gut instinct) at the time a new bet is made.

Similarly, there will be times when you'll ask your Inner CEO for help to manifest a specific outcome, you'll clearly see that you received what you asked for, and you'll continue your movement toward the manifestation of that outcome. This is the equivalent of holding in the game of poker, and it's obviously a fun, exciting, and rewarding place to be.

At other times, you'll ask your Inner CEO for help to manifest a specific outcome, and you'll see that you did not receive what you asked for, even though you crafted a fantastic request for help, you have your code systems worked out with your Inner CEO, you've been astutely managing your master biography files, and you've done everything within your power to manifest the outcome. In these instances, you have to abandon your desired outcome and move in another direction. This is the equivalent of folding in the game of poker, and it's not a situation many people like, although you can shift the unhappy mind-set by fully embracing *The 11th Element* system and philosophy and by understanding that it's really good news.

Still other times, you won't know whether your requested outcome will manifest and whether you should hold or fold. In such instances, you want a strategy for moving through your daily life, reaching clarity on the hold-or-fold options, and knowing what to do in response.

Here is the strategy I use. Follow the guidelines of *The 11th Element* system, craft your requests for help, and send them to your Inner CEO for approval. Completely divorce yourself from an investment in the requested results manifesting at all, looking a specific way, or within your preferred time frame. Go into it understanding that your perspective is limited and what you think is right, best, and would be great for you may or may not be accurate.

You might think, "Easier said than done. How do I reach and maintain a state of detachment like that?" The answer is with intent, discipline, and practice. Developing detachment is the same as developing any other skill. It's difficult and awkward at first, but it gets easier over time with practice. At first, you must discipline yourself to resist any feelings of impatience, anxiousness, disappointment, or attachment—and that may be hard work. Your burden will become lighter, however, if you craft a request and ask your Inner CEO for help developing detachment. Once you begin working with your Inner CEO, you see how things ebb and flow in your world as a result, and you really "get" how limited your perspective is (after seeing numerous examples of the intelligence driving what unfolds for you), detachment becomes much easier, and, ultimately, you create a much more empowered and satisfying state of mind. Then it simply becomes a habit, and the need for conscious effort disappears.

As you cultivate your sense of detachment, you see yourself as preparing to jump one of the gaps that leads to your ideal outcome. You know where you are, you know where you want to be, but you don't know the best way to get there (to jump the gap). So you stand there at the gap and take it one day at a time, remaining alert and open to help coming from any direction. As each day passes, you say to yourself, "Did a door open today that I can walk through to take me closer to my outcome? Is there an action for me to take today? Did I get some sort of sign or signal today?" You just take it one day at a time, watching, waiting, allowing for opportunities to manifest, allowing for information to flow to you, allowing for somebody to come to you, or whatever it might be, keeping all channels open for receiving help from your Inner CEO.

You make decisions or take actions only when you receive knock-me-over-the-head signs, you feel a strong desire to do so, or you actually have a decision point. A *decision point* is a moment when you are actually forced to make a decision or take action. That is, for whatever reason, you're out of time, you're at a fork in the road and must go left or right, someone in a position of authority is requiring a decision and you must comply, and so on. Many people have a tendency to be impatient, and they try to create or force decision points where there really aren't any. That strategy involves great risk.

Think back to the vision of your Inner CEO and the control room working hard to manifest outcomes for you. Imagine your Inner CEO and its staff, running around, sending and receiving e-mails, doing research into the invisible network search engines, negotiating with people, performing due diligence, running simulations, exploring possibilities, and making plans. As we've discussed, the world is a constantly changing place, and what may appear to be the perfect solution, person, idea, resource, strategy, or technique today could change tomorrow. Do you see how allowing more time for your Inner CEO and his staff to work can produce better results? Do you see why you don't want to rush decisions or take actions when you don't actually have a decision point?

When you see signs, receive guidance, notice movements, or reach genuine decision points, if you know exactly what to do and you don't need any help, you make the decision and you take the action. If you're not clear, you use *The 11th Element* system to ask your Inner CEO for guidance on what to do at that specific point. This is what building a successful business and wealth looks like when using *The 11th Element* system. As we discussed, the system is managing a series of gaps where you're taking actions or making decisions, then waiting, then another gap, then another waiting period, and allowing the process to repeat itself until you reach your desired outcome (or something even better).

If you follow this flow and you don't seem to be getting any signs or messages or you don't seem to see any movement at all, only five explanations are possible:

1. Your original request wasn't clear enough or specific enough.

2. The entries in your master biography files are impacting your request.

3. What you want is coming, but the timing isn't right yet.

4. You actually got what you wanted (or something better), but you didn't realize it.

5. Your request was rejected or put on hold by your Inner CEO.

Your Original Request Wasn't Clear Enough or Specific Enough

If you patiently and carefully follow the guidelines for crafting a request for help, this should not be "the problem" for you. But if you don't, it could become a major problem. More times than you might imagine, requests for help that would have been granted fall flat simply because they weren't clear or specific enough. It would happen like this: Your request buzzes off the red fax machine in the control room. Your Inner CEO picks it up, reads it, and says, "I have no idea what you're asking for," then crumples it up and throws it in the trash.

When clients or Ultimate Lifestyle Academy students are just getting started with applying *The 11th Element* system, before they've mastered the art of crafting requests, I often see requests that aren't clear or specific enough to generate responses. So many times, in addition to helping them improve their clarity, I also find myself saying, "You never actually asked for help" or "That's a statement, not a request for help." Following are three request segments that illustrate this point:

1. "My consulting practice is fun and attracts the best and brightest business people in North America to me. These people happily pay me and I happily help them achieve their sales and marketing objectives."

2. "If I'm going to attempt the real estate setup that can be sold, I'm going to need reliable vendors with which to work."

3. "While this is in process, I need to have an income of at least $10,000 monthly to cover living expenses and startup costs. What is the best way to do that?"

The first and second examples make statements but don't actually ask for help and will, therefore, be ignored. The third example makes another statement and then asks a question, but never actually asks for help either, and the author will, therefore, not get what he really wants.

You might think that while the authors make statements and don't actually ask for help, the nature of the help they want is obvious and Inner CEOs ought to respond anyway, but the reality is, they don't. That's not how the system works. Remember, everything is taken literally!

There's also a huge difference between saying "What's the best way to do this?" and "Please *tell me* the best way to do this" or "Help me do this." The differences may appear too subtle to matter, but for Inner CEOs and messages flowing through the invisible network, they have significant impact on the results produced. Because all requests are taken literally, you must actually ask for help.

Many times, when working with intimates at the various companies I've consulted or worked for, people come to me and start talking about one subject or another. After listening for a while, I'll say, "Sorry to cut you off, but do you have a question? Is there an action item *for me* here? Why are you telling me this?" Finally, they'll get to the point and say, for example, "I need your permission to X," "I need you to review Y," or "I need you to talk to so-and-so because they're resisting something we need to get done." Then we quickly get results. The same dynamic operates with requests sent to Inner CEOs all the time, except Inner CEOs don't interrupt you, ask for clarification, or ask you to get to the point. They just ignore your requests.

If clarity and specificity are the only blocks to the manifestation of your ideal outcomes, you can simply rewrite your requests and submit them again. So, if you don't seem to be getting what you asked for, be sure to review your requests to verify that you followed the request-crafting guidelines and that you actually made clear and specific requests for the help you wanted. If you discover that your requests weren't clear and specific enough, rewrite them and submit them again for approval. If you're certain they were clear and specific enough, then move on to consider the following options.

The Entries in Your Master Biography Files Are Impacting Your Request

If you don't seem to be getting what you asked for, it's important to review the guidelines for managing master biography files covered in the previous two chapters. Take a close and honest look at your activities, thoughts, feelings, strategies, and intimates to see if there are opportunities to make changes.

If your master biography files are holding back the manifestation of your outcome, it's either something you can fix or something you must accept and live with. If it's fixable, simply follow the guidelines in the last two chapters, use the techniques, and work with your Inner CEO to change or neutralize the master biography file entries directly or to make changes with the people and activities that are causing the negative or limiting entries in the first place. You must be patient with this process, however, because depending on how complicated the problem is, it could take some time to make the required changes, update the files, and see noticeable changes in the results you produce.

How do you know if master biography files are holding you back or if they can be changed or fixed? Sometimes you'll feel it and you'll just know, especially the more experienced you get with using the system. At other times, you'll suspect a master biography file entry is at work because you'll see a familiar pattern repeating itself, you'll recognize that the repetition couldn't be random, and you'll understand that it must be the result of master biography files. At other times, you'll have to use *The 11th Element* system to craft a request to your Inner CEO asking for help, clarity, and guidance on the subject.

What You Want Is Coming, but the Timing Isn't Right Yet

As discussed in other chapters, many times your Inner CEO and his staff are working on the project for you, and it hasn't manifested yet because they haven't completed their research, due diligence, and planning activities or because the timing isn't right, even if they've completed their work.

As you go forward and begin using *The 11th Element* system, always live by this rule of thumb: The research, due diligence, and planning phases will take more effort than you expect, and the manifestation process will take longer than you think it should.

Remember, the world is a very complex and constantly changing place. It's a big job for your Inner CEO and staff to manage that moving target.

If you apply this rule of thumb and an outcome manifests quickly, you'll be pleasantly surprised. If it takes longer, you're prepared psychologically, and the amount of frustration or disappointment you feel will be eliminated or greatly reduced. The more patient and respectful you can be about the complexity of granting requests and manifesting outcomes, the easier things will be for you and the more fun you'll have on the road to creating business success and wealth.

How do you know if the outcome is on the way and you just need to be more patient? Once you awaken your intuition and get into a rhythm with your Inner CEO, you'll often feel it and you'll just know. At other times, although the outcome hasn't manifested fully yet, you'll have seen enough movement to know it's on the way. And at other times, you'll have to use *The 11th Element* system to craft a request to your Inner CEO and ask for clarity and guidance on the subject. Remember, also, that sometimes all you can do is be patient and wait.

You Actually Got What You Wanted (or Something Better), but You Didn't Realize It

This scenario may play out many times as you work with *The 11th Element* system. You craft a well-written and clear request for help. You keep everything open-ended, including using the wording, "I ask that you give me this or something better." And you actually receive what you asked for or something better, but you won't recognize it. Why? Because you didn't notice or understand the links between the outcome(s) that did manifest and your original requests for help.

Sometimes you won't notice because you're not paying attention to the guidance flowing from your Inner CEO. For example, I once worked with a client whose parents died and left him a valuable piece of real estate. He had to sell the property, and we worked together to craft a request for help to do it. He later called and complained that the house wasn't selling, despite the attractiveness of the property, a talented real estate broker, a healthy market, and many showings. We then worked together to craft a request for help to uncover the cause of the problem and solve it. He continued complaining, however, that the house still wasn't selling, and he wasn't getting any help from his Inner CEO.

After several weeks had passed, we had a long session together during which I asked him dozens of questions. Midway into the session, he told me that he'd been feeling that part of him didn't want to sell the house because his parents had lived in it their entire married lives, both had passed away in it, and he was having difficulty dealing with their loss. He explained that he'd been sensing that part of him felt that if he held onto the house, his parents weren't really gone. I asked him how long he'd been having such feelings and he said, "Three weeks." He also told me that he'd actually received a few offers that were lower than his asking price, but he'd turned them down—something he'd never shared before. It instantly became clear to me that his second request had been granted—his Inner CEO had revealed the source of the problem (a master biography file entry saying he wasn't ready to sell the house), yet he hadn't paid attention to it.

At other times, you may not notice that your request manifested because you forgot you wrote the request in the first place. Many times, I hear about clients who have request boxes full of requests. They go back into the boxes to review them periodically and notice requests they completely forgot they made.

Similarly, you might write a request containing four components for which you want help. You might get help for three of the four components, but ignore that fact because the fourth component was most important to you and you focused exclusively on it. For example, you might craft a single request for help to increase your income to $20,000 a month or more, work 10 fewer hours a week to do it, find several new joint venture partners as part of the strategy, and create or find an additional product or service to offer your customers to support the effort. You might later receive help to reduce your work hours, find the joint venture partners, and create or find the additional product or service, but *not* increase your income to $20,000 or more a month. You might be so focused on failing to increase your income that you forget you actually got help with the other three requests. I see this all the time with clients and students.

Sometimes you won't notice because you're stubbornly attached to the specific outcome you requested or the need for it to manifest in a specific way, and that becomes equivalent to wearing blinders. At other times, you won't notice the links or understand them simply because you never took the time to look.

If you feel that your outcome hasn't manifested and suspect that you may have missed a link, reread your original request; then take a close look at the various outcomes that have manifested to see if you can find one. On many occasions, you'll find one or more links, you'll get a major "aha," and you'll appreciate the brilliance and skill of your Inner CEO at being able to manifest an outcome that's even better than what you asked for. Then it's time to celebrate and enjoy your victory!

If you don't see a link, consider the other options for the reason your outcome didn't manifest, or use *The 11th Element* system to craft a request to your Inner CEO asking for help to see and understand any links you may have missed. This process will prove not only helpful, but tremendously educational.

Your Request Was Rejected or Put on Hold by Your Inner CEO

Few people like this option for obvious reasons, but the reality is that many of your requests for help will be rejected. That will happen because your Inner CEO will look at them *from his broader perspective* and say, "No, that wouldn't really be good for you" or "That would be counterproductive to another project we have in the works." Scenarios like that play out all the time in the corporate arena and should be very familiar to you. When this happens, you'll have no choice but to drop your interest in the outcome that didn't manifest and move on to other projects—in other words, to *fold* and either deal yourself another hand or wait for another one to be dealt to you.

Other times, your requests will still be granted, but at a future date, possibly many years into the future. That will happen because your Inner CEO will look at your requests *from his broader perspective* and say, "That wouldn't really be good for you *now,* but it would be great later." This often happens in the corporate arena, where you'll go to a boss, partner, or board of directors and say, "I'd like the funding and resources to complete X project." The boss, partner, or director will look at it and say, "I see the benefit, but we can't do it right now because we've already committed the budget for this quarter. I'll allocate funding for it in the third quarter." Or, "It looks great, but all of our people are committed right now to launching the new version of our product. I absolutely agree that it would be great for us, but let's table it for now and revisit it after the launch has been completed."

Remember, as frustrating as it might be from one perspective, from another more expanded and empowering perspective, getting a request turned down is actually good news because it means you won't experience a broad-perspective negative outcome that your Inner CEO saw but you didn't. Having a request turned down can also mean that something better will manifest for you later. Getting a "no" or a "later" in this way is truly something to celebrate. After you've been working with *The 11th Element* system for many years and you see how many times you were disappointed in the moment but then saw that something better manifested instead, your mind-set will shift, and it will be much easier to manage the rejections.

How do you know if your request was rejected or put on hold? Again, sometimes you'll feel it, and you'll just know. At other times, you'll see something else manifest and clearly see why it was better for you or why your other request manifesting simultaneously would have been problematic. At other times, you'll have to use *The 11th Element* system to craft a request to your Inner CEO and ask for help, clarity, and guidance on what to do.

What to Do If You Don't Know How to Proceed

There may be times when you ask for help to produce a specific outcome, it doesn't appear to be manifesting, and despite following the suggestions offered, you still won't be clear on the reason or what to do. In such cases, simply use *The 11th Element* guidelines to craft a request for help that communicates this message in your own words and with the details from your own situation. It could read like this: "I asked for your help to produce X. It doesn't appear to be manifesting, and I'm confused about what to do next. Please guide me, give me a sign, give me some clarity, or show me what to do and how to do it. Do I need to improve my request? Is it coming and I just need to be patient? Did I receive something better and didn't realize it? Is there something I need to do to change my master biography files? Did you turn down my request? Please help."

Even the most successful poker players, the ones who win the most hands and money, hold many hands and fold many hands. Holding can be good or bad, depending on the situation. It's just a matter of perspective, just part of the game, and the poker experts do it with the dispassionate perspective of a scientist, as should you.

Holding and folding will be part of your game, too, as you work to build business success and wealth. Armed with your x-ray glasses, your new puzzle pieces, and the tools you've received through the book, you are well prepared to know how and when to hold or fold for maximum advantage.

Are you ready to discover several additional little-known secrets about money, wealth, and business success? If so, turn to Chapter 10.

Wealth as a Destination

All rising to a great place is by a winding stair.[1]
—Francis Bacon, 1561–1626

None of us suddenly becomes something overnight. The preparations have been in the making for a lifetime.[2]
—Gail Godwin

When a spaceship is nearing its destination, it must prepare to dock so that the captain and crew or "away team" can safely disembark and continue their mission. In the previous nine chapters, we focused exclusively on how to apply *The 11th Element* system to create or enhance business success and wealth. You could call that focus *the journey*. In the next two chapters, we continue our discussion of the journey but slowly shift our focus to discussing the destination itself (actually becoming successful and wealthy) so you, too, can prepare for "space dock."

I've studied wealth and success, been wealthy, lost everything, re-created my wealth bigger and better than before, and spent most of my life around wealthy and successful people. During that time, I've learned six little-known but very valuable lessons that I share with you now as part of the preparation for space dock. The six lessons about building business success and wealth are:

1. Most people forget that there are only three ways to do it: Trade your time for it, buy and sell something at a profit (which includes investing), inherit or win a large sum through the lottery or some form of gambling.
2. Money translates into greater freedom, and greater freedom isn't always the best thing for you.
3. It's not going to happen until the best time.
4. Generally, the less you know, the better.
5. Money tends to act as a multiplier, and you must be prepared for the multiplication effect.
6. It's not part of everyone's mission.

Lesson 1: Most People Forget That There Are Only Three Ways to Do It

If you boil it down to its core, there are only three ways to create wealth (to bring a great amount of money into your life):

1. Trade your time for it.
2. Buy and sell something at a profit (which includes investing).
3. Inherit or win a large sum through the lottery or some form of gambling.

Trade Your Time for It

When you give money to someone for something, or someone gives you money for something (in exchange for your time or a product or service), the message being communicated is: "What you offer has value to me, and I'm willing to trade you for it." Therefore, if you're currently in a situation where you trade your time for money, and you want to increase your level of success and wealth, you must find ways of adding more value to the time you have to offer so that people will agree to pay you more in exchange. You can find ways to add more value to your employer with a product or service you sell or almost anything.

On the surface level, you can increase your value through additional education, acquiring new skills, targeting a different niche in the market, raising your fees, adding an additional gift or bonus, or seeking out people who see your value more clearly if you're being underpaid now. Which option is best for you? Send a request for help to your Inner CEO! You can do this on a short-term or long-term basis.

You must be honest with yourself, however, and realize that trading time for money, no matter how much money you receive per hour, is an inherently limiting strategy because there are only so many hours in a day that you can work—or that you're willing to work while maintaining a balanced and happy lifestyle. There are exceptions to this rule, such as when you work for an hourly wage but also receive stock in a company, stock options, or large bonuses. Therefore, if you truly want to create wealth, you'll ultimately want to send requests to your Inner CEO asking for help to find opportunities where you can get stock, options, or large bonuses or for help to transition to the second option: buying and selling something at a profit.

Buy and Sell Something at a Profit (Which Includes Investing)

If you're currently focused on a business-building and wealth-creation model where you buy and sell at a profit, you're in a great place. When using *The 11th Element* system in such a model, send requests to your Inner CEO asking for help to find ways to buy and sell more volume or more profitably—that is, add more products or services, add more value to what you already offer so you can earn more from your product and service sales efforts, or get higher rates of return on your investments.

I have many clients who apply *The 11th Element* system to increase the profitability of their stock and option trading, commodity trading, real estate investing, and other forms of investment. No matter what you focus on, there are always ways to increase efficiency, effectiveness, and the results you produce. Working with your Inner CEO and asking for help is the best method for finding those ways and integrating them into your daily efforts.

Inherit or Win a Large Sum through the Lottery or Some Form of Gambling

Inheritance generally comes from forces outside your control, so there's not much value in applying *The 11th Element* system to request help to inherit money. I do have clients, however, who are applying the system to ask for help with winning the lottery and improving the results they produce from betting on horses, blackjack, sports, and other games of chance. Like anything else, if it's part of your mission or life purpose to win money through such efforts—and many people do earn a great amount of money and become wealthy through them—your requests will be granted. If it's not part of your mission or life purpose, they won't.

Lesson 2: Money Translates into Greater Freedom, and Greater Freedom Isn't Always the Best Thing for You

The more money you have, the more freedom you have, the more options you have, the more choices you have. That can be a good thing or a bad thing. Too much freedom can lead to boredom, lack of motivation, the squandering of time and energy by trying to move in too many directions at once, or getting sloppy in your choices or the execution of your strategies. I've experienced many of these symptoms in my own life and have seen it with many successful people I've known or coached.

Many fortunes and great business successes have been created because of a "fire in the belly" of someone who might have been extinguished or severely weakened if they'd had too much money or too much freedom, for example, Richard Branson, J. K. Rowling, and Colonel Sanders.

If we did not have a phenomenon called *gravity*, our feet would not remain on the ground, and we'd float up and out of control. When astronauts are in space, they must attach themselves to their working or resting areas for the same reason; this is also why the captains and crews of spaceships in the science fiction shows we've discussed have artificial gravity. In all cases, the limiting effect of gravity is positive and necessary to get things done.

Similarly, the limitation that is created by smaller amounts of money is very often a priceless gift because it helps you stay focused and on track as you move toward the fulfillment of your life purpose.

Had I not gone through my Murphy's Law phase, where the lack of money (and the need to get out of debt) severely limited my choices, I wouldn't be where I am now, which I'm extremely pleased about. Had I not gone through other phases where my money supply was limited, I wouldn't have had the motivation to search for and gain the knowledge and skills that later served me so well and continue to serve me today—including the ongoing development and dissemination of *The 11th Element* system. Had I not had times of severe financial limitation that triggered numerous emotional buttons in me that degraded my quality of life and prompted me to search for healing options, I wouldn't have disconnected those buttons, and I wouldn't be the happy, relaxed, and balanced person I am today (although I still have a few more buttons to disconnect!).

During my tough financial times, I always sent requests to my Inner CEO asking for help in turning everything around and bringing more money into my life, but it never happened. Sometimes I was so angry at my Inner CEO that I couldn't think straight. In each case, as I clearly see now, the amount I had was perfect for my mission (at the time) and that I really needed to complete a set of specific and very important learning and developmental lessons for my life purpose. The financial stress caused me to move in specific directions, make certain choices, while avoiding or being blocked from making others.

As I was coming out of my Murphy's Law phase and rebuilding my wealth, I worked on a project that should have returned $10 million or more to me, but instead it returned a much smaller amount. I was angry about getting the smaller amount and felt I hadn't been properly compensated for my time, effort, and level of contribution, but I later realized that had I received the $10+ million at that time, it would have taken the edge off my hungriness, the fire in my belly, and I wouldn't have pursued several other projects that were important to my life purpose. Again, limitation was a blessing to me.

My grandfather wasn't wealthy in his younger days, but he was a successful attorney and financially comfortable when the Great Depression came. Like many other people, he had too much margin debt in his stock trading, lost everything, and went into debt when the stock market crashed in 1929. Rather than go bankrupt like so many other people did, however, he promised his bankers he'd repay every cent he owed—with interest. It took him many years to do that and a great amount of personal sacrifice and sacrifice for his family, but he did it. Repaying his debts aligned with his sense of personal integrity but also paid off when the time came to establish the bank lines of credit needed to help him build Manpower, Inc. Those same bankers were willing to loan him all the money he asked for because they knew he'd repay the loan, no matter what. Who could have guessed in 1929 that his pain would later come back to help him create his greatest success and fabulous wealth?

Always remember that your Inner CEO uses your experiences as raw material just as a sculptor uses clay, a painter uses paint, or a writer uses words—to help you become who you really want to be, to do what you really want to do, think and feel what you really want to think and feel—all on the road to fulfilling your life purpose and completing your mission. Freedom and limitation are parts of the raw material your Inner CEO uses, and they're very powerful tools.

The important thing to realize is that in all scenarios, the presence or lack of money sets specific influences into motion that can have a major impact on your life, mission, and life purpose; therefore, the money flow must be managed very carefully.

Lesson 3: It's Not Going to Happen until the Best Time

My grandfather and Colonel Sanders didn't become wealthy until they were in their 70s. I became wealthy the first time at age 31, then I lost everything and didn't re-create wealth until I was in my 40s. Russ Hobbs, CEO of Blue Ocean Software, became wealthy in his mid-30s. Michael Dell became wealthy in his 20s. If you study success and wealth, you'll see people reaching "the destination" of wealth at different ages.

Ray Kroc was a relatively unsuccessful marketer of restaurant equipment. He didn't sell his first hamburger until age 52. At a time when many people prepare for retirement, he built McDonald's from a handful of hamburger stands into the world's largest restaurant chain—and created great wealth for himself at the same time.

Why did my grandfather and Colonel Sanders have to wait until their 70s? Why did Ray Kroc have to wait until his 50s? Why did I and the others become wealthy at younger ages? Why doesn't everyone get wealthy now or when they want it most? At this point, I think you know the answer: It wasn't part of their mission to do it until they did it—whether they were young or old.

It doesn't matter what you think you want, how anxious or hungry you are, how smart you are, or how lucrative the opportunities that cross your desk may be—if creating business success and wealth are part of your mission and life purpose, they'll come, but not until the best time. And your Inner CEO will be the judge of when the best time is, not you.

Benjamin Disraeli, former British Prime Minister, said it beautifully when he wrote, "The greatest secret of success in life is for a person to be ready when their opportunity comes."[3]

Lesson 4: Generally, the Less You Know, the Better

When I was in my early 20s, I had one of my first readings with an intuitive counselor, Marshall Lever. He said something that I will never forget and that I'd like you to always remember, too: "I can see the life ahead for you very clearly," he said. "It's very positive. You will have worth, a successful career, and more. But I'm not going to tell you any more about what I see."

"Why?" I asked him.

"Because if I said you were going to go to Istanbul to be a gold trader, with your personality, you'd want to go to Istanbul now, and you'd miss out on all the wonderful, magical, and incredible experiences that are necessary to get you there."

Marshall was right. As we've discussed throughout the book, your Inner CEO is working 24 hours a day, 7 days a week to help you complete your mission and fulfill your life purpose. That's a big project and one that spans many years. To get you from birth to the completion of your mission, many projects must be initiated and completed. You can't just zoom to mission accomplished. You must take all the necessary and preparatory steps in between.

In Chapter 2, I discussed life purpose and mission. I also explained that most people don't consciously know what their life purpose and mission are and that it isn't necessary to have that knowledge to be successful. Now you're ready to see, as Marshall Lever so wisely showed me, another blessing is to not know too much about your future.

An example I'm fond of sharing is of a 14-year-old girl named Tara Lipinski, who won the women's figure skating gold medal in the 1998 Winter Olympics. It took a great amount of pain, sacrifice, and hard work for Tara to reach such a high level of achievement, which was clearly part of her mission. But, if Tara had been told at age six that she would win the gold medal just eight years later, that it was her destiny to do it, and she believed it, do you think it might have affected her drive, motivation, commitment, or training regimen? You better believe it would. Having that kind of knowledge in advance would surely have changed things for her.

Just as financial limitation can bring great gifts to you, not knowing too much about your future, mission, or life purpose is an advantage, too. The mystery that is part of life not only allows your Inner CEO to more efficiently guide you from behind the scenes, but also increases the enjoyment of life immensely. Have you ever watched a great movie multiple times? If so, I'm sure you noticed that your enjoyment level dropped each time you watched it because the mystery was gone. Sometimes it's just plain better not to know!

Again, *The 11th Element* concept comes into play in the corporate arena. Meetings take place in companies to discuss subjects that most employees don't know about. There are times in a business structure when you go to a boss or CEO, ask a question about the future direction of the company, and are told that it's confidential. The implication is that such knowledge is available on a need-to-know basis and you don't need to know it to do your job. Keeping such information confidential is essential to the long-term success of the company. It's the same with your life.

Remember, your "job" in this life is to have a more limited perspective and to have the experiences, gather the knowledge, make the contributions, or do whatever else you came here to do as part of your mission and life purpose. Your Inner CEO's job is to have all the knowledge and manage the details to get you to your ultimate destination.

Are you destined to be wealthy? If so, when's the best time? If so, what path will you travel to get there? I don't know, and I strongly suggest that you be thrilled about the fact that you don't know either!

Lesson 5: Money Tends to Act as a Multiplier, and You Must Be Prepared for the Multiplication Effect

This is a trend I've noticed, but it's not a rule or a law. What I've noticed is that if you're basically a happy and balanced person, getting more money will tend to make you happier and more balanced. Conversely, if you're unhappy, what I call *neurotic*, or have many inner demons, getting more money will tend to make you more unhappy, more neurotic, and more victimized by your demons—if such experiences are part of your life purpose and mission.

The first time I was wealthy, I was at my most miserable. That doesn't mean it has to be that way, but my inherent unhappiness and neurosis got multiplied. I know people with very little money and few possessions who are incredibly happy, fulfilled, and serene. I also know people with hundreds of millions who are miserable. It's not the money that creates either reality. It's what's inside us that does it.

It's a well-known and documented fact that people who suddenly become wealthy, whether through inheritance, winning the lottery, getting a lucrative sports contract, becoming a famous musician or actor, or otherwise, have many struggles as a result of the multiplication effect.

This is another reason wealth doesn't come until the best time. For many people, experiencing the multiplication effect is part of their purpose and mission, but for others (including me the second time around), it's not, so the timing of wealth creation must be carefully managed to prevent a major downturn in quality of life.

This is another reason you want to expand the nature of many of your requests to include lifestyle and quality-of-life issues. And it is why, if you know you have issues that could get multiplied, you want to ask for help to uncover and heal their core causes so the multiplication effect has little, if any, negative or limiting impact on you—if and when your wealth comes.

Lesson 6: It's Not Part of Everyone's Mission

You may find this lesson surprising, given the focus of this book, but I feel duty bound to plant this seed within your awareness. Becoming successful in business or becoming wealthy, as you define or dream about it, may not be part of your mission or life purpose.

We live in a world where people can generate hundreds of millions of dollars, even billions of dollars starting with a simple idea they get while shaving or taking a shower. All around us we see examples of unbelievable possibility—people who know how to create wealth and maintain it. The important thing to remember is that none of this is random or accidental. It all comes from intelligent planning from the Inner CEO level as driven by mission and life purpose.

Our culture—books, movies, the media—and many of our parents, mentors, and role models tell us that success means having a great amount of money, fancy stuff, and an expensive lifestyle.

Sometimes our missions have nothing to do with being wealthy. Sometimes we just think we want wealth and abundance because of the incredibly strong cultural programming we received growing up where success, money, and self-worth were so inextricably entwined.

Having a great amount of money, the amount you think you want, or the amount you want when you want it, may not be what you came here to experience—regardless of what you were taught, what you were programmed to believe, or what other people around you are exploring or achieving.

If it's not part of your purpose to have the amount of money you think you want or to have it in your preferred time frame, your Inner CEO will block your moneymaking efforts at every turn—even when you start applying what you've learned in this book. Strategies that are making tons of money for other people won't work for you. Or experiences come into your life (as they did during my Murphy's Law phase) that quickly remove the money you've managed to accumulate—lawsuits, overspending, theft or damage not fully covered by insurance, and so on.

On the other hand, if it's part of your mission and purpose to create business success and wealth, magical things can happen that cause money to flood into your life like a tsunami. If it's part of your mission, you can actually start to feel as though you have the Midas Touch—just by writing simple requests for help and sending them to your Inner CEO.

Fulfilling your life purpose and completing your mission may involve your having a great amount of money, very little money, or experiencing cycles of both—at various points in your life. We're all so different, and unlike what we've been conditioned to believe by society, being rich or prosperous isn't right or wrong, good or bad, spiritual or evil, desirable or undesirable. Nor is it your birthright, a true measurement of your worth and value as a person, or the ultimate goal worth striving for in life and business.

Sometimes, as I mentioned, financial stress is a gift in disguise and you have to flow through it to see what the gift might be. Your life and financial fortunes will unfold as they are meant to unfold—regardless of what you think you want, what strategies or techniques you use, and what society or your peer group says is good, bad, or successful. Here's the bottom line: At any given moment, you'll have only as much money as it takes (or as much as is allowed) to make sure you fulfill your life purpose. No more, no less.

However, because you don't necessarily know—consciously—whether creating wealth is part of your purpose or what the best time for it is, follow the suggestions offered in this book, work with your Inner CEO, and ask for help to produce it—if you feel so motivated. How do you know if it's part of your mission to be wealthy? You will discover the answer to that question by applying *The 11th Element* system and working with your Inner CEO.

In the next chapter, we shift the focus to the destination and begin a discussion of how to be rich.

CHAPTER

11

How to Be Rich

*You are not here merely to make a living. You are here in order
to enable the world to live more amply, with greater vision,
with a finer spirit of hope and achievement. You are here to
enrich the world, and you impoverish yourself if you forget the
errand.*[1]

—Woodrow Wilson

In his book, *How to Be Rich*, J. Paul Getty, the late oil tycoon,
wrote: "I felt that, in our contemporary society, far too much
emphasis was being placed on *getting rich*, on amassing wealth.
Little if any attention was paid to the very important question
of *how to be rich*, how to discharge the responsibilities created by
wealth even while constructively enjoying the privileges and pre-
rogatives conferred by it."[2]

Getty makes a very important point, which is a key part of applying *The 11th Element* system. Many years ago, I participated in a
nine-day, very intensive seminar. One of the stretching exercises at
the event was climbing up a 50-foot telephone pole, figuring out

how to stand on the top (where there was barely enough room for two small feet), then completing the exercise by leaping off the pole to a trapeze that was some 15 to 20 feet away, grasping it, and swinging. I had no problem climbing the pole. I had no problem getting up on top. Once on top, I took a big leap, launched myself forward, and got my hands on the trapeze, but as my weight started to fall downward, I lost my grip and couldn't swing on it, which was the ultimate victory of the exercise.

I wasn't happy with my performance because I wanted the ultimate victory. When I came down, I said to the facilitator, "What happened there? I had enough distance. I had my hands on the trapeze. But I couldn't hold on. Why?" He replied, "It's different for different people, but let me share something with you that I've discovered by facilitating this exercise for many years. The odds are that you were standing on top of the pole and saying to yourself, 'I have to get *to* the trapeze; I have to get *to* the trapeze.' The odds are that you didn't say to yourself, 'I have to get to the trapeze, hold on, and swing.' You were just focusing on getting there. So you got there and that's it."

I thought back on my experience, and it seemed that his analysis was absolutely accurate. I got back up; did the exercise again, focusing on getting to the trapeze, holding on, and swinging; and got the ultimate victory. More importantly, however, I got an important "aha" that I've never forgotten. That is, we often define ideal outcomes for ourselves and focus on producing them, but we rarely focus on or consider what we're going to do when we get there or on why we want to get there at all.

What will you do when you get there? What will you do when you create business success and wealth? What will you do when you use *The 11th Element* system to enhance what you already have? *Why* do you want to get there? You must ask yourself these questions on an ongoing basis and use the system to get help when you receive your answers.

With business success and wealth comes responsibility—to yourself and others. It also brings many new challenges. This chapter focuses on three related topics:

1. Maximizing the benefits received from the wealth and success you create
2. Overcoming the challenges that wealth and success bring
3. Being socially responsible with your wealth and success by helping others

Maximizing the Benefits Received from the Wealth and Success You Create

It's important that you apply *The 11th Element* system to ensure that you, your family, and the other people you care about enjoy and receive maximum *ongoing benefit* from the wealth and success you've created (or are creating). This is similar to *The Lifestyle Imperative* defined in Chapter 4, but it goes beyond it to focus on general quality-of-life issues for you and those you care about. It's important that you apply the system to help yourself and those you care about become as happy, healthy, and fulfilled as possible. We all have a tendency to accept or put up with many negatives in our lives when we could actually make big changes if we focused on changing those negatives.

What can you change inside yourself or outside yourself to improve your overall quality of life? Do you want to keep working and produce the same or better results, but work fewer hours to do it? How about working more flexible hours? Would you prefer to work from home instead of an office? Would you love to take more days off to travel, be with your family, or just plain relax? Would you like to retire and do something different with your time? If so, what would you like to do, and how? Whatever it might be, craft requests for help to do it.

Are there any health issues, major or minor, you've been struggling with? Craft requests for help to uncover the core causes and heal them.

Are there emotional issues you've struggled with—buttons within you that when pushed cause you to feel anger, frustration, sadness, self-doubt, or depression? Do you have fears you'd love to overcome? Craft requests for help to uncover the core causes of the emotional issues you struggle with and heal them once and for all.

What about your relationships—business and personal? Could they use improvement on one or more levels? If so, craft requests for help to uncover the core causes and make changes and improvements.

Is something else dragging down your quality of life? If so, craft requests for help to uncover the core causes and make changes and improvements.

Stuart Goldsmith, a multimillionaire from Great Britain, wrote in his book, *Seven Secrets of the Millionaires:* "The wise person decides how much is 'enough' before setting foot on the path to riches. . . . If you ever make any real money, you will be so caught up in your astonishing success that you will find it very hard to quit. You will be tempted to work harder and faster to get more whilst the going is good. Then, if you hit a lean time, you will work harder and faster to try and get back what you have lost. In short, you will always be working harder and faster. Knowing when enough is enough is the most difficult challenge you will ever face."[3]

"How much is enough?" is a tough question to answer, especially if you're still working to create wealth in the first place. The answer may also change during different phases in your life and in response to other manifestations in your world. But it is a critical question to ask yourself on a consistent basis.

J. Paul Getty wrote about his friend Hal Seymour:

> Hal considered himself to be very wealthy in personal freedom. He was always able to do the things he wanted to do, and always had the time in which to do them. He seldom missed a chance to remind me that, in these regards, I was much poorer than he. Before his death a few years ago, he frequently wrote me letters which opened with the wryly humorous but meaningful salutation: "To the Richest Man in the world from the Wealthiest . . ." I'll have to admit that I envied Hal his abundance of time—which is one of the forms of wealth that people

tend to disregard these days. Rich as I may be from a material standpoint, I've long felt that I'm very poor, indeed, in time. For decades, my business affairs have made extremely heavy inroads on my time, leaving me little I could use as I pleased. There are books that I have wanted to read—and books I have wanted to write. I've always yearned to travel to remote parts of the globe which I've never seen.[4]

In addition to the "How much is enough?" question, here are some additional questions to ask yourself now if you've already arrived at wealth or to keep in mind for your arrival if you're still on the journey:

- Could I live a simpler and less stressed life, and would that serve me?
- Could I work less and do more of the things I want to do?
- If I had more time, what would I really want to do with it?
- Am I caught up in a "more, more, more" loop without being consciously aware of it, without knowing the reason or what's really driving me?
- As exciting as all my affairs and opportunities are, would it make sense to slow down or downshift?
- What is it all for?

This part of the puzzle has become easier for me because on two occasions in my past, I totally exhausted myself from too much push, push, push without enough down time. On one of those occasions, I took a 90-day leave of absence from my job because I felt a bit tired. When I actually stopped working, however, I quickly discovered I had no energy or desire to do anything except watch TV and movies and sleep. It took me a full year of rest to recover from that bout with burnout. With such experiences in memory, it became much easier for me to acknowledge when enough is enough and to make adjustments accordingly.

What about your significant other, family, and friends? How could you help them yourself, or tap into *The 11th Element*, to solve problems, create ideal outcomes they're interested in, resolve health issues, or heal emotional wounds? Be sure to think about the possibilities to help those you care about, those within your sphere of influence, and ask for help as appropriate.

In other words, scan each part of your life and lifestyle (and the lives and lifestyles of those you care about) for areas that aren't optimal, that drag your quality of life down, and that need improvement and use *The 11th Element* system to ask for help to make changes and improvements. That's exactly what I'm doing now and what I've been doing for many years. As a result, I've come light years in terms of how happy I am, how peaceful I am, how many emotional issues I've healed, how much energy I have, how well I sleep, and how many health issues I've resolved (including back pain, acne, high cholesterol, and chronic fatigue). I'm sure you know people or have read about people who created great success and wealth but were unhappy, stressed out, unhealthy, or lonely.

Don't be one of them! Remember that there are no limits to what you can change or create using *The 11th Element* system except those defined by your mission and life purpose. So set your imagination free!

Overcoming the Challenges That Wealth and Success Bring

Once you build your business success and wealth to a certain level, you'll reach *surplus*, which means that you have a consistent surplus of cash and assets. The moment you reach that point, you encounter new challenges, and the larger the surplus, the greater the challenges can be. The more people you have in your orbit (spouse, significant other, children, parents, and other loved ones or people you're responsible for), the more complex it all becomes.

For example, once you reach surplus, you have to develop strategies and create alliances to help you:

- *Invest and grow your surplus.* Find ways of growing your surplus while preserving your base capital and taking only the degree of risk you consider acceptable. So many different investment options these days can get confusing and even overwhelming. Serious mistakes can be made and great losses incurred if the proper strategies aren't discovered and applied.

- *Protect your assets.* The larger your surplus, the greater the need to protect yourself and your assets from lawsuits and other attacks. Specific strategies can be employed in this area, but you must know what they are and how to properly apply them for your own unique situation to receive maximum benefit. If you own expensive assets, you must also protect them from all forms of loss and risk. A friend of mine once went bankrupt because his multimillion-dollar home was destroyed in an avalanche, and it turned out that he didn't have the proper type of insurance to cover the loss.

- *Pass your assets along.* If you have a spouse, significant other, children, or other loved ones to whom you want your assets to go after your death and whom you want taken care of in the event of your unexpected death, you must carefully plan for that eventuality as far in advance as possible. Again, there are specific strategies that can be employed, including specific types of life insurance taken out at specific times, but you must know what the strategies are and how to properly apply them for your own unique situation to receive maximum benefit for all concerned.

- *Minimize the tax you pay.* The more you make and own, the higher the potential tax you must pay. As a business owner, there are many strategies you can apply today that allow you to legally, ethically, and morally pay the absolute minimum possible tax on your income and assets. Again, you must discover what those strategies are and how to properly apply them to your unique situation.

- *Create streams of passive income.* Depending on your situation, personal preferences, and the nature and structure of your wealth, you may want to focus on creating multiple streams of income that are passive in nature, which means that they flow strongly whether you show up for work or not. You can create multiple streams of income through activities such as real estate, investing, network marketing, owning one or more businesses that can run without you, royalties or licensing fees on products you create, and so on.

- *Plan for your retirement.* Again, depending on your situation, personal preferences, and the nature and structure of your wealth, you may want to arrange your affairs to ensure that you and your significant other can retire at your chosen age and still live your preferred lifestyle without stress or worry.

In addition, if you have your own business or businesses, you must make decisions about the optimal legal structure for your affairs. Should they be organized as one or more corporations (and if so, what type?), limited liability companies (LLCs), sole proprietorships, trusts, or a combination of such entities? Depending on the answer, you must also devise strategies for how money flows between the entities and into your bank accounts.

Depending on your unique situation, there may be other challenges you'll face when you reach your desired level of business success and wealth. To get help with these and similar types of projects, you don't want to choose an adviser, investment counselor, stock broker, accountant, tax attorney, life insurance agent, financial planner, or asset protection specialist from the limited perspective of your conscious mind. Get help from your Inner CEO to find the best possible solutions for you and your unique situation. Be sure to use *The 11th Element* system and ask for help as you encounter these kinds of challenges.

Being Socially Responsible with Your Wealth and Success by Helping Others

One of my grandfather's favorite quotes (and a principle he lived by) was written by William James: "The great use of life is to spend it for something that will outlast it."[5]

My grandfather was a generous man who did a great deal to help many people within his spheres of influence. First, he built a company that still exists and still has tremendous impact on the lives of its intimates and the people who use the Manpower services.

He gave his time to causes he considered valuable, gave money away to causes he believed in, and formed a charitable foundation that gave away money for years after his death. He also worked hard to create government reform to help improve the lives of various underprivileged segments of our society. In short, he was a big believer in giving back to the people, communities, and country that helped him create his own wealth and success.

He once wrote, "The total citizen is the kind of person who feels a responsibility for events going on around him. He has emerged from the bud of self-development into the full flow of commitment. He has found that the service motive is as important as the profit motive, and that if the two are mixed in the right proportions, they can literally 'move the earth.' "[6]

J. Paul Getty's father taught him a lesson at a very early age; Getty expressed it this way: "If he's a businessman, the important consideration is what he *does* with his money. As I have said earlier, the best use he can make of it is to invest it in enterprises which produce more and better goods and services for more people at lower cost. His aim should be to create and operate businesses which contribute their share to the progressive upward movement of the world's economy, and which thus work to make life better for all. Therein lies the justification for wealth, and therefrom does the working businessman derive the greatest satisfaction."[7]

If you have a business, it touches one or more communities where it operates. You have the opportunity, by applying *The 11th Element* system, to request help to improve the quality of life in the communities where you have impact. All you have to do is ask!

Do you have intimates who helped you on the road to creating your business success and wealth? If so, how could you use your personal resources or tap into *The 11th Element* to help them? You could use the system to craft requests that include wording such as: "I want to achieve the following goals in my business, but to do it, I also want to touch the lives of my intimates in as many positive ways as possible. Please help me do that, too."

When Blue Ocean Software was sold, the CEO, Russ Hobbs, in addition to cashing out stock options and paying the other legal obligations of the business, gave large bonuses to the employees who contributed most to the success of the company. Some of the bonuses were enormous. Others were relatively small. The more an employee contributed, the larger the bonus.

Russ was in my office one afternoon and said this about the impact those bonuses had: "I had no idea what kind of impact that money would have. People started coming into my office and telling me what they did with it. They helped nieces or nephews go to college. They helped mothers and fathers have operations, buy houses, and take trips. They helped their friends and children in all kinds of ways. Watching how the money moved and the impact it had was amazing."

Would you like to give some of your surplus away to charity or a worthy cause? If so, maybe you're already passionate about specific ones. Or, you can use *The 11th Element* system to ask for help to find the causes that resonate best with who you really are and have the most positive impact. There are so many people, projects, and causes that need funding and that could make such a positive difference in the world if they received some of your surplus.

Giving to charity is not a must or something everyone *should* do, regardless of the degree of surplus they've created. But I do believe in giving back and having positive impact on the world, whatever shape it takes. My goal is to have tremendous positive impact through this book and the other aspects of my work, and giving back through your chosen occupation is certainly one way to do it. You can also have tremendous positive impact on the world by just focusing on doing what you do best or doing what you can do within your own sphere of influence: kids, friends, associates, acquaintances, intimates, company, community, and so on.

There are so many ways to give back and help others. When drafting your requests, ask for the help you want and need for yourself, and always remember to ask for help in having as much positive impact on others as possible and finding as many ways as possible to have positive impact.

Does giving back seem far away to you because you're under financial pressure right now, you have a mountain of debt you need to pay off, or you barely have enough income to pay your bills at the moment? No problem. Just keep it in mind. The idea is to keep a watchful eye on what you'd do when you do create your business success and wealth. That's the point of this chapter—to start thinking about it now, before you jump off the pole and head for the trapeze!

Remember that if your Inner CEO wasn't already working on impacting the lives of others in positive ways through your efforts and you don't ask for help to do it, it isn't going to happen. But if you ask, it opens the door to a possibility that might not otherwise have manifested—a possibility that could help many people. So be sure to ask!

Being socially responsible with your wealth not only helps other people and gives you joy, satisfaction, and pride (if these are emotions that are important to you), but also, if it is genuine and from the heart, it modifies your master biography files in very positive ways. It's like adding an entry that says, for example, "This person is in business because she wants to serve her customers well, create wealth for herself and help her loved ones, and have as much positive impact on the quality of life on the planet as possible." Can you see how such master biography file entries could have tremendous positive impact on the results you produce? Remember what my grandfather said about combining the profit and service motives.

My journey has included all the components I discussed in this chapter—creating business success and wealth, maximizing the benefits received from it for myself and for those within my sphere of influence, overcoming the challenges wealth and success can bring, and being socially responsible with the wealth I've been able to create.

I've seen how much fun and rewarding each component can be, as well as how challenging. Therefore, I decided to create the Ultimate Lifestyle Academy to offer resources for others wanting to travel along a similar road. The program has various levels that focus on helping people create wealth, manage it, grow it, structure their financial and business affairs, improve their quality of life, and find ways of contributing and giving back. If you're interested in learning more, visit http://www.ultimatelifestyleacademy.com.

The message is simple: Resist the temptation to focus only on what it will take to *get* rich. Keep a watchful eye on *how to be rich*—now that you have a clear understanding of what that means—and apply *The 11th Element* system to help you *be* as rich as possible.

The final step in our journey together is to give you your marching orders—the specific steps to take right now to help you get as much benefit as possible from the book.

CHAPTER

12

Executing *The* 11th Element

Success is a journey . . . not a destination.[1]

—Ben Sweetland

W e've come a long way together. You now have all the new *11th Element* puzzle pieces I promised. You've added them to the pieces you acquired before we met, and a powerful and exciting new picture and map have popped into view for you that will guide you toward the level of wealth and success prescribed by your life purpose and mission. You began our journey with *ordinary vision,* and now you have *x-ray vision* that will allow you to see what many others do not—what's going on behind the scenes and the true nature of the engine that actually drives the creation of business success and wealth.

Whenever you learn something new or get your perspective widened, the biggest challenge comes when you try to bridge the gap among new ideas, new information, new intentions, and *implementa-tion*. It's a huge gap, but it can be easily bridged when it comes to *The 11th Element* system if you take a few simple and immediate steps after finishing this book. I call those steps *your marching orders*.

A term used in the self-help and success-training industry, the *suntan effect*, describes the phenomenon that occurs after reading a book, listening to a tape set, or attending a seminar, then getting all pumped up and excited (the equivalent of going out in the sun and getting a tan), but ultimately returning to your daily life and seeing all the excitement fade with no lasting impact (the equiva-lent of your tan fading).

I want to have lasting impact on you. I'm not interested in giv-ing you a suntan. I want to help you begin your march toward ap-plying *The 11th Element* in a *consistent, ongoing* way to produce extraordinary results, in less time, with less effort, and much more fun. In this chapter, I share a few additional insights, reinforce some of the key *11th Element* concepts, and give you several simple and immediate steps to take after you finish this book to begin building your momentum.

No matter what result you want to produce in your business and wealth-building efforts, you have several strategy choices. You can try to do it all by yourself—based on what you can see and process from the limited perspective of your conscious mind and intellect. But, as you've seen, that's an extremely limiting option. You can rely on ex-perts and other people, and what they can see and process from the limited perspective of their conscious minds and intellects. But, as you now know, that, too, is a flawed and extremely limiting option.

You can move forward using *the random approach*, where you go on about your business and hope that your requests for help will somehow make it onto the desk of your Inner CEO and that the guidance and messages your Inner CEO sends to you somehow make their way into your conscious awareness. Certainly, there are examples of people who have succeeded and built wealth using the random approach, but, as Robert Allen wrote in the foreword, sys-tems and toolkits save you time, energy, and money.

Or, you can proactively apply *The 11th Element* system to tap into the tremendous raw power available through your Inner CEO and the invisible network to find the people, ideas, resources, techniques, and strategies that can help you most—on a daily basis.

Which option will you choose? If you choose to proactively apply *The 11th Element* system, you must draw a line in the sand and never cross back over it into the old way of doing things. You must make a commitment to use the system, work with your Inner CEO, and make your "dance steps" as effective, efficient, smooth, and elegant as possible.

You don't want to try to build business success and wealth with blinders on or one hand tied behind your back. You want your eyes wide open. Tap *all* the resources and power available to you by applying *The 11th Element* system to every aspect you get involved with for starting businesses; building businesses; running businesses; finding and taking advantage of opportunities; avoiding pitfalls; and building, managing, and preserving your wealth. You also want to keep a constant and watchful eye on the impact your efforts are having on your health, emotional well-being, happiness, stress level, relationships, family life, and the lives of those you care about, while applying the system to ask for help in making appropriate changes and improvements as needed.

How to Receive Immediate Benefit from *The 11th Element* System

Steps to take immediately after finishing this book are:

1. *Set up your system for sending messages to your Inner CEO.* You may decide to use a request box, a folder on your computer, or some other method for sending requests for help to your Inner CEO. Regardless of which option you choose, physically set it up, write a letter to your Inner CEO to let her know what you chose and what to monitor going

forward, and send the letter to your Inner CEO using the message-sending system you chose.

2. *Choose your "at-the-moment" signal.* You want to be able to send requests for help to your Inner CEO at the moment you want or need help, so the next step is to choose your unique but easily identifiable signal. Then write a letter to your Inner CEO to let her know what you chose and what to monitor going forward. Send the letter to your Inner CEO using the message-sending system you chose in Step 1.

3. *List all the projects you want help with.* As discussed in Chapter 4, scan your present situation and make a list on paper of all the projects, wants, needs, and problems you'd like help with *right now*. Take your time, really think hard about it, and be as thorough as possible.

4. *Prioritize your list.* Take all the items on the list you created in Step 3 and prioritize them according to importance. Rank them by which ones would have the most impact on your business, wealth building, and quality of life if they manifested *right now*.

5. *Add one more item to the top of your list.* After you compile and prioritize your list, add another item and put it at the number one position. This will be your request for help from your Inner CEO to do everything in her power to help you fully understand and apply *The 11th Element* system, master each component, and receive maximum benefit going forward.

6. *Review the request-crafting guidelines.* Review the guidelines to make sure you're crystal clear on each one, so that each request you craft has the greatest odds of being approved and manifesting. Either copy the guidelines from Chapter 4 or visit my web site to print a summary: http://www.11thelement.com/guidelines.html.

7. *Craft four initial requests for help.* Choose the top four items on your list (including the number one request described

in Step 5 as the first one), and craft requests for help with each. You can craft additional requests later, but start with and focus clearly on your top four only.

8. *Send your four requests to your Inner CEO for approval.* Using the method you chose in Step 1, send your first four requests to your Inner CEO for approval, then let go of any attachment to when, how, or if the outcome will manifest.

9. *Patiently wait for signs, signals, movements, action, and decision points.* When your requests are approved, there will be movement in your world. Patiently wait for it while being consistently open-minded and alert.

10. *Make decisions and take actions.* When your decision-making and action-taking points arrive—and they will—make the decisions, take the actions (or ask for help if you're not clear), and continue your journey at warp speed toward full manifestation of your ideal outcomes.

11. *Use your in-the-moment signal as appropriate.* Whenever you need help in the moment, remember to use your signal and ask for the help you need. It's easy to forget, but so powerful and impactful when you remember!

12. *Commit to investing the time and energy to become masterful.* Applying *The 11th Element* system is a skill, and like any other skill you discover for the first time, it takes time to get fully comfortable, enhance your skill level, and ultimately become masterful. Make a commitment now to invest whatever time and energy is required to achieve mastery.

13. *Tell your intimates.* If you have intimates in your business (now or in the future), when you feel comfortable enough to do it, be sure to educate them about *The 11th Element* so they can apply the system, too. By doing that, you increase the amount of power available to you for manifesting your ideal outcomes. Not everyone will resonate with this material or be willing to apply it consciously, but the

more people that do, the better for all concerned. In addition, share the system with friends and loved ones.

14. *Review the key concepts until they become second nature.*
Repetition is the mother of skill, so reread the entire book
often, especially Chapters 4, 5, and 6, until applying the
system becomes *installed* in you at the deepest level—so
you use it automatically, without thinking about it, like a
habit. You can also visit the following page on my web
site to print simple summary sheets of the key concepts:
http://www.11thelement.com/concepts.html.

15. *Celebrate your victories, and be at peace with delays and "rejections."* So many people, including me, often forget to
take the time to celebrate their victories and spend too
much time focusing on problems or the next task. Take the
time to celebrate your victories, to really feel the joy that
comes from getting a request approved and manifested and
from producing extraordinary results, and allow yourself
the luxury of being as peaceful as possible with delays and
rejections.

16. *Use your X-ray glasses.* Take advantage of every opportunity you can to put on your X-ray glasses and study the
success stories of others from the perspective of *The 11th
Element*—whether by reading articles, listening to interviews, reading biographies, or asking others to tell you
their stories. This will reinforce your excitement about
the system and your motivation to continue applying it
until your results help create a *self-motivation cycle.* You
might consider starting a journal to make notes of things
you noticed when using your X-ray glasses in your life and
the lives of others. You could also take notes on the various signs, signals, messages, and movements you noticed
in your own life in response to your requests for help.
Such a document might prove valuable and fascinating in
the years to come.

17. *Continue asking for help by slowly working through your list.* As you feel so motivated, move beyond the initial four requests for help by crafting requests for help with the other items on your list. Move slowly but surely, and pace yourself. Consider crafting a request asking for help to time the additional requests so you don't overload yourself with trying to interpret too many movements, signs, and signals at once when you're just getting started with the system.

18. *Have fun with the system.* Any pathway to creating business success and wealth can have moments of difficulty, frustration, confusion, and pain. But when you truly embrace *The 11th Element* concepts and system, everything becomes much lighter, easier, and more fun—even the tough times. And the lighter, more fun, and easier things get, the higher your quality of life rises.

When you actually follow and apply these 18 steps, you'll discover that they take only a short time to complete. They will help you build momentum and confidence in the system, and the *lifelong benefits* you receive will far outweigh your small investment of time and energy.

Your Inner CEO Is Always Working to Help You

This completes our journey together into the *The 11th Element*. I hope the journey has left you changed in multiple and profound ways. I hope it has motivated you to begin traveling down a new and different road toward the creation of business success and wealth in your life. I hope it has motivated you to consider both the journey and the destination and to focus on both *getting* rich and *being* rich.

You will never again need to feel alone on your travels or as you work to manifest your ideal outcomes, because you now know that your Inner CEO and her staff of assistants are by your side 24 hours a day, 7 days a week, working hard and doing everything possible to help you—every step of the way.

You never again need to use incomplete or generic strategies, because you now know how to find and attract people, ideas, resources, techniques, and strategies that are customized, personalized, and optimized for your unique situation, personality, wants, needs, mission, and life purpose.

Apply *The 11th Element* system to the best of your ability. Continue applying the system even when things are going extremely well for you. Remember to focus on results *and* lifestyle outcomes and stay flexible and open-minded. Enjoy your journey as much as possible, while always seeking to help as many other people as you can along the way.

Thank you for spending this time with me. I wish you great success in all that you do. Be well. . . .

A

Resources

The following information allows you to contact the people discussed in this book and tap into many of the resources mentioned. Web sites are listed instead of other contact information because of frequent changes.

My Web Sites

You can visit the following web sites to learn more about my work and other tools and resources I recommend and endorse:

http://www.11thelement.com
http://www.ultimatelifestyleacademy.com
http://www.bobscheinfeld.com
http://www.kennedysite.com
http://www.directmarketingtools.com

http://www.advertising-marketing-breakthroughs.com

http://www.masteryofemotions.com

http://www.terrydeanmarketing.com

http://www.livingtheultimatelifestyle.com

Awakening and Developing Your Intuition

For additional resources to help you awaken and develop your intuition, visit this page on my web site:

http://www.11thelement.com/intuition.html.

Intuitive Counselors

Consider intuitive counselors to help you receive messages from your Inner CEO and through the network as you work to develop your own skills. Intuitive counselors can also help uncover negative master biography file entries that may be impacting the results you produce. For a list of recommended intuitive counselors, visit:

http://www.11thelement.com/intuitives.html

Healers

For a list of healers who can help you uncover and edit negative files on the spot, visit:

http://www.11thelement.com/healers.html

Managing Master Biography Files

I'm always testing, developing, and adapting new techniques and resources to help uncover and process master biography file entries.

To get on my mailing list so you can stay up-to-date with my latest techniques, visit:

http://www.11thelement.com/mbf.html

Guidelines for Crafting Requests

To print a quick summary of the guidelines for crafting requests, visit:

http://www.11thelement.com/guidelines.html

Key Concepts Review

Visit the following page on my web site to print simple summary sheets of the key concepts of *The 11th Element* system:

http://www.11thelement.com/concepts.html

Shaina Noll

If you're interested in learning more about my sister's music, you can visit her web site at:

http://www.shainanoll.com

Bob Serling

Bob helps companies—ranging from independent inventors, to small businesses, to Fortune 500 corporations—develop new products and improve the marketing of their products. Visit him at:

http://www.Product-Lab.com

Bill Harris

Bill offers an extremely powerful personal growth system to help you accelerate your mental, emotional, and spiritual growth. Visit:

http://www.11thelement.com/billharris.html

Lynn Robinson

Lynn is an author, speaker, and intuition consultant who can help you communicate with your Inner CEO and tap into the invisible network for information and guidance. Visit:

http://www.lynnrobinson.com

Robert Allen

Robert is my friend, associate, and mentor on book publishing. To stay up-to-date on his wealth-building resources, visit:

http://www.robertallen.com

Howard Schultz and Starbucks

http://www.starbucks.com

Richard Branson and the Virgin Group

http://www.virgin.com

Wendy's

http://www.wendys.com

Marriott

http://www.marriott.com

Robert Kiyosaki

Author of *Rich Dad/Poor Dad:*

http://www.richdad.com

Nike

http://www.nike.com

Dell

http://www.dell.com

Harry Potter

http://www.harrypotter.com

Reebok

http://www.reebok.com

Kentucky Fried Chicken (KFC)

http://www.kfc.com

The Avatar Program

http://www.avatarepc.com

How to Uncover and Neutralize Negative Files

This appendix describes various techniques you can use to uncover and neutralize negative files, starting with the simplest
and graduating to the more complex. You can use some of the
techniques by yourself, while other techniques require a partner or
will be more effective if used with a partner.

Before explaining the techniques, there are four points I want
to make crystal clear:

1. *Uncovering and working with negative files take time and effort.* These techniques aren't magical, although they can appear
that way. Negative files can be uncovered and neutralized quickly
and easily, or they can be somewhat elusive and have layers that

must be peeled back over time. What's the bottom line? Be patient. The rewards are well worth it!

2. *Life purpose and mission are still the driving forces.* If it's not part of your life purpose or mission to uncover or change negative files at this particular moment (or at all), it's not going to happen, no matter how hard you work or what technique you use. Like everything else, your Inner CEO will monitor your activities; evaluate them against your mission, purpose, and active or queued projects; and allow only active file changes that are truly in your long-term best interest. In addition, negative files started being created when you were born, and they have been continuously created ever since. They'll be created every day going forward by your daily thoughts, feelings, and activities. Regardless of their origination date, negative or limiting ones are often used by your Inner CEO to help you fulfill your life purpose and complete your mission. Negative files often act as brakes, speed controls, detours, and on ramps and off ramps for "highways" you can take to manifest your ideal outcomes (discussed in detail in Chapter 10). Even if you don't personally like their negative or limiting impact, negative files often bring great gifts, just as request rejections do. When the time comes that those negative files are no longer necessary, however, your Inner CEO will work with you to change or neutralize them. That's when the techniques I'll share with you will have the most impact.

3. *Don't let the simplicity of the techniques fool you.* As you'll see, while it can take some time and effort to use the techniques and follow through to get a complete result, they're basically very simple and powerful!

4. *Your best choice is always to send a request for help to your Inner CEO.* Despite the power of the techniques included in this section, your best solution is always to send a request for help to your Inner CEO to uncover and neutralize negative files. I offer the techniques because one or more of them may be the exact tools your Inner CEO would choose to use to help you, and I want you to have quick and easy access to them.

Template for Neutralizing Negative or Limiting Master Biography File Entries (Negative Files)

This is the basic template I use for myself, for clients, and for students when I write requests for help neutralizing negative files:

Dear _____:

I've been working to achieve _____, but I just don't seem to be getting anywhere. I suspect that master biography file entries might be blocking my progress.

If that's correct, and if it's in alignment with my mission and life purpose to change the entries at this time, please help me yourself or guide me to the people, ideas, resources, techniques, and strategies I can use to uncover the entries having impact; then change, heal, release, or neutralize them so they no longer have any negative or limiting impact on me.

From the limited perspective of my conscious mind, this is what I think I want, and I ask that you give me this or something even better.

[Signature]

Following are the techniques I use myself and recommend to clients and students. We begin with techniques for uncovering negative files; then we continue to techniques for neutralizing them.

Negative File Uncovering Technique 1: Enhance Your Requests for Help

You can actually work to uncover and neutralize negative files each time you craft your requests for help. This is actually a 12th guideline for crafting requests that I saved for this discussion of master biography files. As a "PS" in your requests, or in the main body of your letters, you can add wording such as this: "If there are any negative files that could limit me from getting the outcome I've just asked for, to the extent that you can control it, please help me change those files or help neutralize them from having any negative or limiting impact on producing the outcome I'm asking for."

Your Inner CEO and the staff members in the control room are very smart and have access to tremendous amounts of information, but they can't track every single negative file without something to narrow their focus. There are too many files! They might not know about every negative file that could have impact on you in advance, but if you add wording as suggested to your requests and a request is approved, they will look for all negative files that could impact that request. You can view this as an insurance policy.

Inner CEOs don't lie or distort the truth. If there are truthful entries in your files that could have negative or limiting impact on you, they may not be fixable. For example, if your company is in financial trouble and may not be able to keep its doors open another four weeks if something doesn't change immediately, the entries may not be fixable unless your situation changes. If your product or service doesn't genuinely solve the problem or meet the need it claims to, the files may not be fixable unless you change products or services. If you have serious problems with your service department, customer service, or technical support and it will take six months or more to solve them, the files may not be fixable until the problems are actually solved.

Many times, however, the negative files are fixable if a "That's true, but . . ." comment is added to the files, or if you adjust your behavior, strategies, or the content of your surface communications. This is why you want to ask for help with negative files in all your requests to your Inner CEO.

Negative File Uncovering Technique 2: The Magic Question

Ask yourself: "What kind of file(s) would have to be active in the network for me to get the result I'm getting?" For example, in my mid-20s, I noticed a pattern repeating. I would be working at various jobs or on my own projects, I'd be successful, then get more successful, then even more successful; just as I was about to have an enormous breakthrough, something would pop out of nowhere and I'd self-destruct and have to start over.

That pattern repeated itself five times until I discovered and neutralized the negative files at work by asking that question and using the other techniques offered later in this appendix. I discovered that when I was a child, I saw my father create tremendous financial success, but from my limited perspective, he did it at too great a cost—health problems, two divorces, tremendous anger and stress in his daily life, and strained relationships with me, my brother, and my sister. Through those years, a negative file was created (approved by my Inner CEO because it contributed to fulfilling my life purpose) that said something like this: "Don't let him get too successful or he'll hurt everyone around him, including himself."

There was a time when I had a pattern of being ignored whenever I went into public places—by waiters, waitresses, salespeople, gas station attendants, store clerks—everybody. Everywhere I went people ignored me, even though I saw them taking excellent care of others (so it wasn't that they were busy and that anyone would have waited the way I did).

By seeing this pattern repeat itself, I realized negative files were at work in my relationships. Because the pattern was so strong and so consistent, I realized there had to be negative files in the invisible network saying something like, "Ignore this guy."

Do you have strong and consistent patterns you're struggling with? If so, what type of negative files would have to be active to create them?

Negative File Uncovering Technique 3: Ask People Who Are Close to You

Sometimes other people hear you saying things repeatedly or see you acting in certain ways, and they see negative files in action even though you don't see them yourself. If you're creating something in your life you don't like or failing to produce a result you want and you suspect a negative file is at work, ask people around you if they've noticed your saying or thinking something on the subject that could reveal the existence of one—or a clue to the existence of one.

Negative File Uncovering Technique 4: Take an Elevator Ride

This technique can be very powerful and a lot of fun, too. Choose a problem, want, or need that is being blocked by a negative file. Close your eyes. Take a few deep breaths. Visualize yourself entering an elevator. Imagine and feel the elevator going down 10 floors. See the floor counter on the top center of the elevator as it counts down the floors. When you get to the bottom, the elevator door opens onto a long hallway with many doors on the left and right and one door at the end.

Walk down the hallway looking at the doors until you see one with these words written on it: "The negative file that's stopping me from getting X." Make sure you're willing to enter the room and find out what's blocking you. If you aren't, leave and try again at another time. If you are willing, open the door, enter the room, and know that inside is a person who'll talk to you, or a symbol, or something that will give you insight into the negative file that's active—or at least start the ball rolling.

It may take you some time or thought to decode the message if it's symbolic, but I've seen this technique work almost like magic. It's often most effective if done with a partner who talks you through the steps, asks you questions about what you discover in the room, what it means to you, and so on.

Negative File Uncovering Technique 5: *Throw Up!*

This technique may seem strange or uncomfortable at first, but I assure you it works! I learned this from Dr. Bernie Gunther. Think about an outcome you want very much—the outcome a negative file seems to be interfering with. Notice how it feels to be blocked when you want it so much. Feel the blockage as much as you can. Then lean forward, actually make the sound of vomiting, and imagine that a bunch of "stuff" comes out of your mouth and flies to the floor in a pile. Look at the pile of "stuff" and ask yourself, "What's in there?"

Flow with the first thing that comes to mind. You may notice a parent saying something to you, a belief, a negative thought pattern, anything. Everyone is different. The "stuff" is generally the content of the negative file that has been hurting you—or a strong clue about where to find it.

Negative File Uncovering Technique 6: *Ask a Good Intuitive Counselor for Help*

As I mentioned in Chapter 6, there are gifted people who genuinely have the ability to tap into the invisible network and/or "talk" to your Inner CEO to receive valuable information about you. I call such people *intuitive counselors*. If you feel a negative file is limiting you, a reading with a good intuitive counselor can be the quickest way to uncover it. To get the most recent list of intuitive counselors I've personally worked with and can recommend without hesitation, visit this page on my web site:

http://www.11thelement.com/counselors.html

Negative File Uncovering Technique 7: The Magic Book

I use this technique all the time and love it. Many years ago, I created an imaginary mountaintop retreat consisting of a rectangular building with several rooms off a central hallway. One of the rooms is designed to help me work with negative files. I close my eyes and go into a meditative state by doing some deep breathing and body relaxation. Then I find myself in the central hallway of my retreat, and I enter the negative file room. Inside the room on a tall wooden stand is a book—a leather-covered, antique-looking, big, heavy book.

I walk up to the book and say out loud in my imagination: "Please let me know what negative files, if any, are in the way of my getting X in my life." Then I simply flip through the pages in my imagination until I feel drawn to open to a specific page and read what's there. The writing on the page will reveal the nature of the negative file that's in the way—if there is one.

Negative File Uncovering Technique 8:
The Magic Statements

On a blank piece of paper, make the following statement to yourself or say it out loud to yourself or a partner:

"My father used to say about money . . ."

or

"My father used to say about wealth . . ."

or

"My father used to say about success . . ."

Then fill in the blank with whatever comes into your mind. Resist the temptation to judge, edit, think, or analyze what comes out. Just write down or have your partner write down whatever comes to your mind. Do it in a free-flow manner—no thinking, no editing.

Continue to make the statement, "My father used to say about . . ." and continue filling in the blank with whatever comes into your mind and writing what you "hear" until nothing more comes to mind and you feel complete.

Then repeat the same process but say: "My mother used to say about _____ . . ."

If someone other than your father or mother had a strong influence on you as a child or in your financial life, do the same exercise but replace "father" or "mother" with the name of that person or add the person to mother and father and do additional rounds.

I've done this process in seminars and with private clients, and I'm always amazed by the breakthroughs this simple technique creates for people. They consistently come up with negative files they never consciously thought about before but that have been causing much damage.

Neutralizing Negative Files

Sometimes simply becoming consciously aware of negative files causes a breakthrough, and they release on the spot. But if you need to go further, try the following techniques. First, as always, the most powerful option is to send a request for help to your Inner CEO. Your request might read like this:

Dear _____:

I just discovered a negative file that I believe is interfering with my ability to _____.

Here it is: _____. [Describe the nature of the negative file.]

Please help me yourself or guide into my life the people, ideas, resources, techniques, and strategies I can use to uncover the core cause of that negative file, and release, heal, or change it so it no longer has any negative or limiting impact on my life.

From the limited perspective of my conscious mind, this is what I think I want, and I ask that you give me this or something even better.

[Signature]

Second, there are gifted people who can help you not only uncover negative files (such as intuitive counselors) but also actually change or neutralize them on the spot. I call such people *healers*. To get the most recent list of healers I've personally worked with and can recommend without hesitation, visit this page on my web site: http://www.11thelement.com/healers.html.

Third, after you discover negative file(s) using these techniques, write them on a piece of paper; put the paper into a bowl, container, or fireplace; and burn it. Carefully and intently watch the paper until it turns to ash and the flame dies out. Burning has very powerful symbolic meaning to your Inner CEO and your staff of assistants—it gives a very clear message: "Release this!"

If you used the *Magic Book Technique*, here's what you do in your imagination: Read the page, then forcefully rip the page out of the book, put it into a big ceramic bowl in the center of the room, then create a torch or some sort of burning device (I use a high-tech laser pistol), and set the pages on fire with it. As it burns, make the mental statement: "Release this" or a similar affirmation (if you feel so moved), and watch the paper burn until the flame completely dies out.

After the paper has burned, write what you want to be seen instead of your negative files on a blank page you find in the book. Then you repeat the process. You flip through the pages in the Magic Book again, open to any other pages you feel drawn to read in your search for negative files, read them, rip them out of the book, put them into the bowl, burn them while affirming their release, and then write their replacements. You keep repeating the process until you no longer feel drawn to read any more pages.

When working with negative files, there are two possibilities—the content of the file is true, but you want to add a "Yes, but . . ." to it, or the active file isn't true any more, and you want to add a new entry. Here are both scenarios:

1. *Adding a "yes, but . . ." to the file.* Suppose you have a great product, but your company is struggling financially. Maybe the survival of your business is in jeopardy. Suppose that's the negative file you discovered by reading the page in your Magic Book—that people aren't buying from you because the negative file is causing people to worry about your company's stability. In this example, you might write on your new page: "Yes, it's true that our company is having financial difficulties right now. But that doesn't change the fact that our product truly delivers on our promises (and then some) and the fact that even if something did happen to our business, we have a relationship with Acme Service Company, who will service the product and provide support according to the terms of our contract. Finally, we really want this business to succeed and would appreciate your help by becoming one of our customers. We promise we'll work very hard to service and support you and to make sure you get the exact benefits you're buying our product to receive."

2. *Changing the actual file contents.* Suppose you discovered an active file that said, "No, don't buy from me because then my business might be successful, and I don't deserve to be successful." In this case, you might write the following on your blank page to replace it: "I now deserve to be successful no matter what I may have believed in the past."

You get the idea. You can't change negative files if they're true, but you can either add information, preferably heartfelt, or change them if they're no longer true. If you choose to use a technique other than the Magic Book, simply craft a request for help to your Inner CEO and ask for help to add the "Yes, but . . ." statement or for help to change the actual file contents.

When working with negative files, like everything else in *The 11th Element* system, you must be patient, trust your Inner CEO, and remember: Fast isn't always better!

The following two techniques combine the uncovering and neutralization phases of working with negative files.

Negative File Uncovering Technique 9: Let's Play a Game of Pool

Anytime you say something, do something, or something happens in your world, specific psychological responses click into gear and generate a response of some kind: a thought, a feeling, an action, or something else. This process is often called *programming* or *conditioning* in the self-help and psychological literature.

It can be very useful to stimulate your programming and psyche in various ways to reveal negative files that may be buried within you. When a negative file is in place that conflicts with or opposes a desire or want you have, your desire and the negative file collide with each other and bounce off in different directions.

Think about the game of pool. You use a cue stick to hit ball number 1 so it strikes ball number 2 and causes it to move in a particular direction—to roll into the pocket.

Working to uncover negative files using this technique is a similar process. You want to use the "cue stick" of your desire to strike ball number 1 (what you want to create or change in your life) so it strikes ball number 2 (a negative file that conflicts with it) and causes it to move in a particular direction—to "roll" into your conscious awareness so you can remove it.

This technique is designed to help you cause a "collision" that reveals the negative file at work.

A variety of options are included so that you can choose the best one(s) for you. Try whichever one(s) appeal to you—or try all of them—to see what works best for you. You can also adapt them into new techniques that you like better or that work better for you.

Each option has three steps:

1. *Create the collision.* You can do this by speaking out loud or writing on a piece of paper.

2. *Notice the negative file that bounces to the surface.* Always write this information on paper.

3. *Edit or neutralize the negative file.* This is handled in various ways that are explained in Chapter 7 and in the previous section of this appendix (Neutralizing Negative Files).

To begin the process, simply choose one thing you really want to change or create in your life and refine it to a simple, one-line statement. For example: "I will earn $150,000 or more this year doing work I love."

Keep the statement short and simple so you can deliver it repeatedly (verbally or in writing) without having to think about it or refer to notes. I call this your *simple statement.*

Remember, your goal is to create collisions that reveal negative files, so, going back to our pool analogy, you want to strike "balls" in various ways to do that. Here are a few options to try:

- *Forcefully make your simple statement in writing or out loud.* For example, write on paper or say out loud: "I will earn $150,000 or more this year doing work I love." Then monitor your thoughts and feelings and see if the statement collided with a negative file. Write down what you notice or hear. For example, you may hear, "No way. That's too much money too fast." Or you may hear, "There's no way I'll ever make that kind of money next year." Or you may feel an emotion, such as fear, anxiety, or something else. Whatever it is, *write it down* on your paper. *Repeat the process* until you can make your simple statement and hear, see, or feel nothing in response.

- *Forcefully state the problem.* For example: "I can't make as much money as I'd like because . . . ," and you then monitor your thoughts and feelings to see what kinds of collisions get created and how your mind fills in the blank. Again, *write down what you notice* and *keep repeating the process* of stating, noticing, and writing until you can make your simple statement and get nothing in response.

These techniques can also be done with a partner. When doing them with a partner, the process is similar. The partner simply asks you to forcefully make your simple statement or to forcefully state the problem.

Then you do it, and the partner asks you if anything surfaced in your awareness and writes down what you say. The partner keeps asking you until you say that nothing came up.

Negative File Uncovering Technique 10: The Ultimate Partner Technique

I adapted the following technique from something I learned when I went through the Avatar program many years ago.

As before, the idea is to create collisions that reveal negative files. But this technique takes things one step further.

Often, when you use the techniques described previously, negative files come to the surface, you release them, and you are on your way.

The additional power here is that sometimes a negative file—or clues to finding a negative file—take nonverbal forms, such as a feeling, a body movement, an eye twitch, and so on.

It's more difficult to work with or release such nonverbal cues without help because you may not notice them. But a partner will. As strange as it may seem, simply by working with the nonverbal cues themselves, you can often release the negative files once and for all.

To prepare for this process, as before, take one thing you really want right now and refine it to a simple, one-line statement—your simple statement. Then follow these steps:

1. *Make your simple statement.* Your partner does this by saying to you: "Make your simple statement."

2. *Look for collisions.* After you make your statement, your partner asks you: "Any negative files?" This means: "Did any words or feelings or something else float into your mind just after the statement was made?" You respond with a yes or no and explain what you experienced. Your partner also notes anything he or she observes or senses. The negative file can be something you say to yourself, a feeling, a muscle twitch, a slight rise in your left shoulder, an eye blink—anything showing or hinting that something "collided" with what you want.

3. *Your partner writes down the negative files that surfaced.* Your partner writes down all the negative files he or she notices or hears from you.

4. *Start the release process.* The next step can feel very awkward at first—but please do it anyway because it can be so incredibly powerful. Exaggerate whatever came up. If a negative file came up as the statement: "There's no way I'll make that kind of money this year," you make that statement repeatedly, exaggerating the feeling of it, the energy of it, the tone of voice you heard in your head—every aspect of it. Exaggerate

everything! If a body movement came up as the negative file, exaggerate that, too. If there was a slight eye blink, make the eye blink *big and dramatic* and repeat it again and again. If it was a slight rise in your left shoulder, exaggerate it! Make it a *huge* rise in your left shoulder. Keep exaggerating whatever came up repeatedly—for as long as it takes for you to feel that the charge or emotional edge is gone from it. As I said, this may be uncomfortable or embarrassing and it may take a while, but it's very important. Stretch, have fun, and know you're giving yourself a great gift.

5. *Go back and check.* After you finish the exaggeration process and you feel that the charge may be off the negative file, your partner repeats the process to test if the negative file has been released. Your partner again says, "Make your simple statement." You make your statement. Your partner then asks, "Same negative file?" If yes, repeat Steps 3, 4, and 5 until you get a no. Once you get a no, move on to Step 6.

6. *Repeat the process until you feel clear.* Go back to Step 1 and repeat the steps until no other negative files surface. Most likely, more negative files will come up when you use this process.

7. *Burn the paper on which your partner wrote everything down.* Burn the paper over a safe receptacle. And if it feels right to you, use this affirmation before you touch the flame to the paper: "As this paper burns, so shall all these limiting thoughts, feelings, beliefs, and negative files be completely released forever."

NOTES

Introduction

1. Albert Einstein, Periodical booklet. *Bits & Pieces* (Chicago: Ragan Communications, 2002).
2. Albert Einstein, *The Columbia Dictionary of Quotations*, ed. Robert Andrews (New York: Columbia University Press, 1993), p. 614.

Chapter 1: Networking with the Ultimate "Inside Contact"

1. Henry David Thoreau, Periodical booklet. *Bits & Pieces* (Chicago: Ragan Communications, 2002).
2. Antoine De Saint-Exupery, *The Little Prince*, translated by Katherine Woods (New York: Harcourt Brace Jovanovich, 1943).
3. James Wallace and Jim Erickson, *Hard Drive: Bill Gates and the Making of the Microsoft Empire* (New York: Harper Business, 1992), p. 109.

Chapter 2: The Wild Card Is Always Dealt

1. François-Marie Voltaire, Periodical booklet. *Bits & Pieces* (Chicago: Ragan Communications, 2002).

2. George Bernard Shaw, Periodical booklet. *Bits & Pieces* (Chicago: Ragan Communications, 2002).
3. Richard Bach, *Illusions: The Adventures of a Reluctant Messiah* (New York: Dell, October 1994), p. 159.
4. Charles Schulz, Periodical booklet. *Bits & Pieces* (Chicago: Ragan Communications, 2002).
5. David R. Thomas, *Dave's Way: A New Approach to Old-Fashioned Success* (New York: Berkley Books, 1992), p. 72.

Chapter 3: Why the 10 Elements Don't Work

1. G. K. Chesterton, Periodical booklet. *Bits & Pieces* (Chicago: Ragan Communications, 2002).
2. David R. Thomas, *Dave's Way: A New Approach to Old-Fashioned Success* (New York: Berkley Books, 1992), p. 3.
3. J. Paul Getty, *How to Be Rich* (New York: Jove Books, 1965), p. 197.
4. See note 3, p. 198.
5. See note 3, p. 198.
6. Michael Dell, *Direct from Dell: Strategies That Revolutionized an Industry* (New York: HarperBusiness, 1999), p. 33.

Chapter 4: The Rules of the Game

1. Christopher Morley, *Dictionary of Quotable Definitions*, ed. Eugene E. Brussell (Englewood Cliffs, NJ: Prentice-Hall, 1970), p. 553.

Chapter 5: Turbocharging Your Engines

1. Franz Grillparzer, Periodical booklet. *Bits & Pieces* (Chicago: Ragan Communications, 2002).

Chapter 6: Making the Jump to Warp Speed

1. Jean Blomquist, Periodical booklet. *Bits & Pieces* (Chicago: Ragan Communications, 2002).
2. Albert Einstein, Periodical booklet. *Bits & Pieces* (Chicago: Ragan Communications, 2002).
3. Ken Blanchard, *The Logic of Intuitive Decision-Making: A Research-Based Approach for Top Management*, ed. Weston H. Agor (New York: Quorum Books, 1986), on dust jacket.
4. Weston H. Agor, *The Logic of Intuitive Decision-Making: A Research-Based Approach for Top Management* (New York: Quorum Books, 1986), p. 28.
5. See note 4, preface, viii–viv.
6. See note 4, p. 3.
7. See note 4, p. 7.
8. See note 4, p. 34.
9. Michael Dell, *Direct from Dell: Strategies That Revolutionized an Industry* (New York: HarperBusiness, 1999), p. 127.
10. Mick Brown, *Richard Branson: The Authorized Biography* (London: Headline Books, 1998), p. 246.
11. J. B. Strasser and Laurie Becklund, *Swoosh: The Unauthorized Story of Nike and the Men Who Played There* (New York: Harper-Business, 1991), p. 114.
12. David R. Thomas, *Dave's Way: A New Approach to Old-Fashioned Success* (New York: Berkley Books, 1992), p. 57.
13. See note 12, p. 68.
14. See note 12, p. 93.
15. See note 12, p. 93.
16. J. Paul Getty, *How to Be Rich* (New York: Jove Books, 1965), p. 14.
17. Sandra Weintraub, *The Hidden Intelligence: Innovation Through Intuition* (Boston: Butterworth-Heinemann, 1998), p. 18.
18. See note 17, p. 97.
19. See note 17, p. 106.
20. Arthur Fry, Periodical booklet. *Bits & Pieces* (Chicago: Ragan Communications, 2002).

21. Nathaniel Hawthorne, Periodical booklet. *Bits & Pieces* (Chicago: Ragan Communications, 2002).
22. Richard Paul Evans, *Inside the Best Sellers* (Traverse City, MI: Rhodes & Easton, 1997), p. 33.
23. James Redfield, *Inside the Best Sellers* (Traverse City, MI: Rhodes & Easton, 1997), p. 45.
24. Marc Shapiro, *J. K. Rowling: The Wizard Behind Harry Potter* (New York: Griffin, St. Martin's Press, 2000), pp. 48–49.
25. See note 24, p. 49.
26. Howard Schultz, *Pour Your Heart into It: How Starbucks Built a Company One Cup at a Time* (New York: Hyperion, 1999), p. 25.
27. See note 26, pp. 36–37.
28. See note 26, p. 52.
29. Charles Goodyear, Periodical booklet. *Bits & Pieces* (Chicago: Ragan Communications, 2002).
30. Lynn Robinson, Electronic newsletter, reprinted with permission of the author.
31. James Wallace and Jim Erickson, *Hard Drive: Bill Gates and the Making of the Microsoft Empire* (New York: HarperBusiness, 1992), p. 51.
32. See note 30, p. 22.
33. See note 9, p. 7.
34. See note 9, p. 11.
35. See note 9, p. 10.
36. See note 9, p. 14.
37. Bob Serling, Personal letter to the author, reprinted with permission.
38. Bill Harris, Personal letter to the author, reprinted with permission.
39. Marlo Thomas, *The Right Words at the Right Time* (New York: Atria Books, Simon & Schuster, 2002).

Chapter 7: Is Anything Flying beneath the Radar?

1. Jim Rohn, *Excerpts from the Treasury of Quotes* (Rocklin, CA: Prima, 1994), p. 8.

Chapter 8: Going beyond Salespeople, Marketing, and Word of Mouth

1. Aaron Scheinfeld, Personal conversations with author and personal writings.
2. Henry Ford, Periodical booklet. *Bits & Pieces* (Chicago: Ragan Communications, 2002).
3. Malcolm Gladwell, *The Tipping Point: How Little Things Can Make a Big Difference* (Boston: Back Bay Books, Little, Brown and Co., 2000).
4. Emanuel Rosen, *The Anatomy of Buzz: How to Create Word-of-Mouth Marketing* (New York: Doubleday Books, 2002).
5. Michael Dell, *Direct from Dell: Strategies That Revolutionized an Industry* (New York: HarperBusiness, 1999), p. 20.
6. See note 5, p. 32.
7. Howard Schultz, *Pour Your Heart into It: How Starbucks Built a Company One Cup at a Time* (New York: Hyperion, 1999), p. 81.
8. See note 7, p. 245.
9. See note 7, p. 248.
10. See note 7, p. 251.
11. See note 7, p. 6.
12. J. W. Marriott and Kathi Ann Brown, *The Spirit to Serve: Marriott's Way* (New York: HarperBusiness, 1997), p. xii.
13. See note 12, p. xiv.
14. See note 12, p. xvii.

Chapter 9: Knowing When to Hold or Fold Your Hand

1. Eden Phillpotts, *The Forbes Book of Business Quotations: 14,173 Thoughts on the Business of Life*, ed. Ted Goodman (New York: Black Dog and Leventhal Publishers, 1997), p. 937.
2. George S. Patton, Periodical booklet. *Bits & Pieces* (Chicago: Ragan Communications, 2002).

Chapter 10: Wealth as a Destination

1. Francis Bacon, *Dictionary of Quotations*, ed. Bergen Evans (New York: Delacorte Press, 1968), p. 291.
2. Gail Godwin, Periodical booklet. *Bits & Pieces* (Chicago: Ragan Communications, 2002).
3. Benjamin Disraeli, Periodical booklet. *Bits & Pieces* (Chicago: Ragan Communications, 2002).

Chapter 11: How to Be Rich

1. Woodrow Wilson, Periodical booklet. *Bits & Pieces* (Chicago: Ragan Communications, 2002).
2. J. Paul Getty, *How to Be Rich* (New York: Jove Books, 1965), preface, p. vii.
3. Stuart Goldsmith, *Seven Secrets of the Millionaires* (Berkshire, England: Medina, Ltd., 2001), p. 129.
4. See note 2, pp. 210–211.
5. William James, *The International Dictionary of Thoughts*, eds. John P. Bradley, Leo F. Daniels, and Thomas C. Jones (Chicago, J. G. Ferguson Publishing Company, 1969), p. 444.
6. Aaron Scheinfeld, Personal writings.
7. See note 2, p. 196.

Chapter 12: Executing *The 11th Element*

1. Ben Sweetland, Periodical booklet. *Bits & Pieces* (Chicago: Ragan Communications, 2002).

INDEX

ACKNOWLEDGMENTS

Like any other achievement or result, this book would never have been conceived and born had it not been for the contributions of many other people.

The most important thank you must go to my grandfather, Aaron Scheinfeld, who started teaching me the core principles of *The 11th Element* system when I was 12 years old, and whose achievements and philosophies continue to inspire me on a daily basis.

Special thanks must also go to my agent Michael Broussard whose feeling about me and this book caused him to take me on as a client, helping me realize my lifelong dream of being published by a major New York publisher.

I'm also very grateful to my editor at John Wiley & Sons, Airié Stuart, who instantly recognized the value of *The 11th Element* and shared her excitement with Michael and me with such strength that we felt she was the best possible editor for the project.

Robert Allen went way beyond the call of duty by helping me brainstorm ideas to shape the proposal that sold the book, writing the Foreword, and continuously inspiring me by his example and achievements within the world of publishing.

The title for this book, *The 11th Element,* came from the creative brilliance of my friend Randy Gage during a mastermind session he conducted in Costa Rica. Thanks, Randy!

Special thanks must also go to my associate Amanda Smith. By doing such a great job of managing the nuts and bolts of my Internet businesses, she gave me the time and peace of mind to pursue many other projects, including this book. Thanks, Amanda!

Without the manuscript "massaging" and formatting help Brian Bevirt gave me, I would never have met my deadlines. Thanks, Brian, for all your help and support.

My friend Dale Novak is a gifted graphic artist and photographer who did a terrific job of working with me to design the illustrations for the book. Thanks, Dale, for your talent and contributions.

I'm profoundly grateful to my wife Cecily for her wise and valuable contributions to the book, plus her consistent support and tolerance of the many somewhat challenging aspects of my creative process. I love you, Beauty. None of this would be as sweet without you.

I'd also like to thank my daughter Ali and my son Aidan for joining Cecily and me, helping us form our perfect little family, and for giving me ongoing inspiration to create and contribute.

I also want to thank the thousands of clients, students, friends, and associates who each contributed in their own unique and valuable way to the creation and refinement of *The 11th Element* system.

Finally, I'd like to thank and congratulate *you* for finding your way to this book. It's not an accident, and tremendous value will come from our interaction in one way or another. Thanks for spending your time with me here!

ABOUT THE AUTHOR

For more than 10 years, Bob Scheinfeld has been helping individuals, entrepreneurs, managers, and executives increase their profits and catapult their sales, all while making dramatic improvements in their quality of life. His business experience includes creating profitable million-dollar businesses (on and off the Internet), packing self-improvement seminars with eager audiences, building Blue Ocean Software into an "Inc. 500" fastest-growing company three years in a row, and having a bird's-eye view of how his grandfather grew a small business, Manpower, Inc., into a multibillion-dollar Fortune 500 powerhouse.

Bob's story of becoming a stressed-out millionaire, his plunge into $153,000 of debt, and his surge up to become a millionaire again with balance and joy in his life, is compelling and inspiring. But most important to you is the method he used to make this transformation.

He developed a simple system that brought him from the depths of despair, confusion, anger, and desperation to success and fulfillment in his business and personal life. Driven to share the benefits of this gift, he has taught his system to tens of thousands of people in more than 100 countries. The ongoing success of everyone who applies his system qualifies Bob as an undisputed expert in the arenas of business achievement and personal fulfillment. Using these experiences and more, Bob knows how to help you produce extraordinary results, in less time, with less effort, while having a lot more fun.

Bob Scheinfeld is committed to your business success and your ability to fulfill your life's purpose. Bob writes from his home in Virginia, where he lives with his wife Cecily, his daughter Ali, and his son Aidan.